~ At a Glanc

Paragraphs

FIFTH EDITION

Lee Brandon
Mt. San Antonio College

WADSWORTH
CENGAGE Learning™

Australia • Brazil • Japan • Korea • Mexico • Singapore • Spain • United Kingdom • United States

WADSWORTH
CENGAGE Learning™

To Sharon

At a Glance: Paragraphs
Fifth Edition
Lee Brandon

Senior Publisher: Lyn Uhl

Director of Developmental
English and College
Success: Annie Todd

Development Editor:
Karen Mauk

Assistant Editor:
Melanie Opacki

Editorial Assistant:
Matthew Conte

Media Editor: Amy Gibbons

Senior Marketing Manager:
Kirsten Stoller

Marketing Coordinator:
Ryan Ahern

Marketing Communications
Manager: Stacey Purviance

Content Project Manager:
Aimee Chevrette Bear

Art Director: Jill Ort

Print Buyer: Susan Spencer

Rights Acquisition Specialist:
Katie Huha

Production Service: Books By
Design, Inc.

Cover Designer: Walter Kopek

Cover Image: Getty Images

Compositor: S4Carlisle
Publishing Services

For product information and technology assistance, contact us at
Cengage Learning Customer & Sales Support,
1-800-354-9706

For permission to use material from this text or product, submit
all requests online at **www.cengage.com/permissions.**
Further permissions questions can be emailed to
permissionrequest@cengage.com.

Library of Congress Control Number: 2010933766

ISBN-13: 978-0-495-90629-2
ISBN-10: 0-495-90629-8

Wadsworth
20 Channel Center Street
Boston, MA 02210
USA

Cengage Learning is a leading provider of customized learning solutions
with office locations around the globe, including Singapore, the
United Kingdom, Australia, Mexico, Brazil and Japan. Locate your
local office at **international.cengage.com/region**

Cengage Learning products are represented in Canada by Nelson
Education, Ltd.

For your course and learning solutions, visit **www.cengage.com.**
Purchase any of our products at your local college store or at our
preferred online store **www.cengagebrain.com.**

Printed in the United States of America
1 2 3 4 5 6 7 14 13 12 11 10

~ Contents

iii

Preface

In this, the fifth edition of *At a Glance: Paragraphs*, the surf writer, gallantly perched on a pencil, once more celebrates the "flow of writing." Like waves at a beach, writing is cyclical, moving forward and backward and forward again. The surf writer will always be searching for the "perfect wave," meaning the best possible expression. The recursive movement of writing and rewriting is the essence of good writing. Instruction in this book—comprehensive, flexible, relevant, and stimulating—is predicated on that systematic, relentless revision.

At a Glance: Paragraphs is the second-level book in the *At a Glance* series. Along with *At a Glance: Sentences*, *At a Glance: Essays*, and *At a Glance: Reader*, it meets the current need for succinct, comprehensive, and up-to-date textbooks that students can afford. All four books provide basic instruction, exercises, and writing assignments at the designated level, as well as support material for instructors. *At a Glance: Sentences* and *At a Glance: Paragraphs* include a transition to the next level of writing. *At a Glance: Paragraphs*, *At a Glance: Essays*, and *At a Glance: Reader* each ends with a handbook that students can refer to for help with sentence-level issues or for problems with mechanics. *At a Glance: Reader* presents brief writing instruction and thirty sources for instructive writing demonstrations, critical thinking, discussion, and reading-based writing. Each book in the *At a Glance* series can be used alone, with one of the other *At a Glance* books, or with another textbook. Two or more *At a Glance* books can be shrink-wrapped and delivered at a discount.

Comprehensive Coverage

Using instruction with exercises, examples, and writing applications, the Fifth Edition of *At a Glance: Paragraphs*

- focuses on paragraph writing with the option of writing short essays (Chapters 1–13);
- features the writing process with attention to prewriting, organization, writing, revision, and editing—each phase illustrated with student examples (Chapters 1–2);

- includes instruction for using the Writing Process Worksheet, an optional one-page form that guides student work through the stages of exploring the topic, organizing the writing, and writing (blank Writing Process Worksheet for enlarging and copying following the Student Overview on page xx and on the Instructor and Student Companion Sites);
- incorporates professional and student writing in instruction on how to read critically and how to write summaries, reactions, and two-part responses (Chapter 3);
- for instructors who give one or more short essay assignments with paragraph assignments, uses student paragraphs and essays to show how the same basic organizational techniques employed in developing essays can also be employed in developing paragraphs (Chapter 4);
- leads students through nine patterns of paragraph writing, each with instruction, student and instructor examples of paragraphs (40 altogether, 8 of them new to this edition), and an abundance of writing prompts and topics covering reading-based, general (often keyed to model student and professional examples), cross-curricular, and career-related subjects, with each chapter including a pattern for organization while recognizing that a specific pattern is seldom used alone (Chapters 5–13);
- features a handbook that addresses sentence-level issues, such as subjects and verbs, fragments, comma splices, run-ons, sentence combining, verbs, pronouns, modifiers, punctuation, capitalization, and spelling (Chapter 14);
- and supports handbook instruction with an abundance of material on the Companion Sites for students (exercises, additional instruction, worksheets, documentation guides, and so on) and for instructors (syllabi, teaching suggestions, and additional aids).

⌒ Instructional Approach for Writing Paragraphs

The instruction in *At a Glance: Paragraphs* is concise and direct. Each of Chapters 5 through 13 uses the same sequence: a writing strategy for a particular pattern, a box of transitional terms, an exercise that gives students practice in organizing the pattern, student examples and professional examples with questions for students to answer and discuss topic suggestions (reading-based, cross-curricular, career-related, and general topics) for writing such paragraphs or short essays, and a concluding summary of guidelines specific to the pattern.

New and Enhanced Material

- Eight reading selections, of 40 selections altogether
- More third person, objective reading selections
- Mode-specific boxed transitional words in nine chapters
- An enhanced Writing Process Worksheet, designed to provide guidance for students and save time and effort for instructors
- Additional instruction, writing topics, and writing prompts on reading-based writing as the summary, reaction, and two-part response, showing how students can write with more substance and become better prepared to write across the curriculum
- Anti-plagiarism instruction with simple application of MLA 2009 documentation
- A revised Chapter 4 with fresh examples showing the basic similarity of well-developed paragraphs and well-developed essays
- Examples of documented student writing
- Additional topics and prompts that can be used for either paragraphs or short essays
- APA Guide for writing research papers, available on the *At a Glance* Student and Instructor Companion Sites
- An enhanced Self-Evaluation Chart to help students track their needs and goals and promote self-reliance

Special Brandon Features at a Glance

The Writing Process Worksheet

The Writing Process Worksheet provides a flexible, systematic approach to specific assignments and leaves a word trail so that instructors can help students confront problems during the exploration and planning of assignments and reconstruct what went right and wrong after the paper is written. This classroom-tested form can save students and instructors time and effort, and produce effective results. A copy of the worksheet is located in the textbook following the Student Overview, on the Student Companion Site, and on the

Instructor Companion Site. It is discussed in detail in Chapters 1, 2, and 3. Instructors who require this sheet can ask their students to photocopy the generic version from the Student Companion Site or enlarge and copy it from their textbook. They can also customize the Word copy on the Instructor Companion Site to fit their pedagogy or particular assignments.

Reading-Based Writing

Reading-Based Writing as an Option: Because this book does focus on writing paragraphs of all types, instructors whose pedagogy favors assigning mostly personal narratives will continue to find *At a Glance* hospitable and effective. However, this book now has another instructional dimension as an optional approach: **reading-based writing**. Instructors who wish to help students transition from personal experience to more analytical thought with reading-based writing have choices that include: (1) beginning with the personal narrative and phasing in reading-based writing; (2) interspersing reading-based writing with other assignments; or (3) using reading-based writing throughout the course. Students who work with reading-based writing will be able to function better in writing across the curriculum and move more smoothly into advanced courses.

Reading-Based Writing Defined: Reading-based writing requires students to read a source, write an analytical reply, and give credit to the originator for the ideas they borrow and the words they quote. Credit can be noted formally (MLA with 2009 Update in this book—or with APA form, as presented on both the Student and the Instructor Companion Sites) or informally (by using clear references with acknowledged credit and quotations with quotation marks), depending on the instructor's preference. As for structure, reading-based writing can be a summary, a reaction (paragraph or essay), or a two-part response (with separated summary and reaction). Although the reaction can include personal experience to clarify and support conclusions, the text should be at the center of the writing. The reaction can also incorporate summary to convey a broad aspect of the text. But summary is never the major concern of the reaction, although the summary is a useful assignment in teaching students to identify main ideas, to organize thoughtfully, and to avoid plagiarism.

∿ Support Material for Instructors

- **Instructor's Guide for *At a Glance*.** The Instructor's Guide—available both in print at Cengage Learning, Higher Education, at 800-354-9706 and online at the Instructor's Companion Site—provides helpful hints for teaching *At a Glance* in the classroom. It includes sample syllabi; suggestions for working with basic writing students and ESL students; grading tips; Answer Keys; quizzes on sentence writing, handbook material, readings; and more.
- **Instructor Companion Site for *At a Glance*.** This instructor site provides helpful resources in addition to the Instructor's Guide, such as PowerPoint slides, at login.ccngage.com.
- **Student Companion Site for *At a Glance*** at www.cengagebrain.com. The student site provides helpful resources such as sentence writing exercises, a 2009 MLA Guide and an APA Guide to documented papers, a printable Writing Process Worksheet, tips on writing resumes and letters of application, additional reading selections, and more.

∿ Acknowledgments

I am profoundly indebted to the many instructors who have reviewed *At a Glance: Paragraphs* for these five editions and helped it grow and remain fresh and innovative. Here are a few of those thoughtful and imaginative reviewers: Cheyenne Adams, Genesee Community College; Shirley Dubman, Jefferson College; Laura Gray-Rosendale, Northern Arizona University; Matt Mathesius, Columbia Basin College; Cindi Clarke, Belmont Technical College; Tim Kelley, Northwest-Shoals Community College; Darin Cozzens, Surry Community College; James Crooks, Shasta College; Marilyn Black, Middlesex Community College; Thomas Beverage, Coastal Carolina Community College; Deborah Burson-Smith, Southern University at New Orleans; Joanna B. Chrzanowski, Jefferson Community College; David Lang, Golden Gate University; Phyllis MacCameron, Erie Community College; Kathy Masters, Arkansas State University; Richard Pepp, Massasoit Community College; and Steve Stremmel, American River College. Thanks also to members of the English Department at Mt. San Antonio College for their helpful suggestions.

I also deeply appreciate the expert, dedicated work of freelance principal editor Karen Mauk, production manager Nancy Benjamin with Books By Design, editorial specialist Ann Marie Radadiewicz, permissions editor Maria Leon Maimone, and my colleagues at Cengage Learning: Annie Todd, Kirsten Stoller, Katie Huha, Matthew Conte, Melanie Opacki, Stacey Purviance, Ryan Ahern, Courtney Morris, and Aimee Chevrette Bear.

I am especially grateful to my family for their cheerful, inspiring support: Sharon, Erin, Michael, Kathy, Jessica, Debora, Shane, Lauren, Jarrett, and Matthew.

Lee Brandon

Student Overview

This book is designed to help you write better paragraphs and short essays. Chapters 1 and 2 focus on the writing process itself. You'll discover prewriting techniques to help you get started, and you'll learn ways to develop, revise, and edit your drafts until you produce polished compositions. Chapter 3 explains how to read critically and write summaries and critiques of reading selections. Chapter 4 discusses the essay in relation to the paragraph and can help you expand some of your paragraphs into essays.

Each of Chapters 5 through 13 describes a different pattern for developing an effective paragraph. Chapter 5, for instance, is about narration; Chapter 6 is about description; Chapter 7 is about exemplification—that is, the use of examples. All of those chapters include sample paragraphs written by students and professional writers. Throughout, questions and exercises help you practice what you have learned. Chapter 14 is a handbook to which you can refer when you need assistance in grammar, usage, sentence structure, punctuation, and capitalization.

Following are some strategies to help you make the best use of this book and to jump-start the improvement in your writing skills.

1. **Be active and systematic in learning.** Take advantage of your instructor's expertise by being an active participant in class—one who takes notes, asks questions, and contributes to discussion. Become dedicated to systematic learning: determine your needs, decide what to do, and do it. Make learning a part of your everyday thinking and behavior.

2. **Read widely.** Samuel Johnson, a great English scholar, once said he didn't want to read anything by people who had written more than they had read. William Faulkner, a Nobel Prize winner in literature, said, "Read, read, read. Read everything—trash, classics, good and bad, and see how writers do it." Read to learn technique, to acquire ideas, to be stimulated to write. Especially read to satisfy your curiosity and to receive pleasure. If reading is a main component of your course, approach it as systematically as you do writing.

3. **Keep a journal.** Keeping a journal may not be required in your particular class, but, regardless of whether it is required, jotting down your observations in a notebook is a good idea. Here are some ideas for daily, or almost daily, journal writing:

- Summarize, evaluate, or react to reading assignments.
- Summarize, evaluate, or react to what you see on television and in movies, and to what you read in newspapers and magazines.
- Describe and narrate situations or events you experience.
- Write about class content in other courses and career-related matters you encounter in other courses or on the job.

Your journal entries may read like an intellectual diary, a record of what you are thinking about at certain times. Keeping a journal will help you to understand reading material better, to develop more language skills, and to think more clearly—as well as to become more confident and to write more easily so that writing becomes a comfortable, everyday activity. Your entries may also provide subject material for longer, more carefully crafted pieces. It is important to get into the habit of writing something each day.

4. **Evaluate your writing skills.** Use the Self-Evaluation Chart inside the front cover of this book to list areas you need to work on. You can add to your lists throughout the term. Drawing on your instructor's comments, make notes on matters such as spelling, word choice, paragraph development, grammar, sentences, punctuation, and capitalization. As you master each problem area, you can check it off or cross it out.

Here is a partially filled out Self-Evaluation Chart, followed by some guidelines for filling out your own.

Self-Evaluation Chart

Spelling/ Word Choice	Paragraph Development	Grammar/ Sentences	Punctuation/ Capitalization
separate	topic	fragment 188	comma after long
a lot	sentence 11	run-on 189	introductory
studying	use specific	parallel	modifier 205
boundary	examples 87	structure 203	periods and
avoid	support 22–23	subject-verb	commas inside
slang 22		agreement 195	quotation
			marks 205

- *Spelling/Word Choice.* List words marked as incorrectly spelled on your assignments. Master the words on your list and add new words as you accumulate assignments. Also include new, useful words with their brief definitions and comments on word choice, such as avoiding slang, clichés, and vague or general words.
- *Paragraph Development.* List suggestions your instructor made about writing strong topic sentences and attending to matters such as coherence, language, unity, emphasis, and support.
- *Grammar/Sentences.* List problems such as subject-verb agreement, sentence fragments, comma splices, and run-ons. If you tend to begin sentences in the same way or to choose the same patterns, use your chart to remind yourself to vary your sentence patterns and beginnings.
- *Punctuation/Capitalization.* List any problems you encounter with punctuation and capitalization. Because the items in this column may be covered in Chapter 14, you can often use both rule numbers and page numbers for the references here.

5. **Take full advantage of the *At a Glance* Student Companion Site and other technology.** Using a computer will enable you to write, revise, and edit more swiftly as you move, alter, check, and delete material with a few keystrokes. The Student Companion Site offers additional exercises and instruction. Many colleges have writing labs with good instruction and facilities for networking and researching complicated topics. The Internet, used wisely, can provide resource material for compositions.

6. **Use the Writing Process Worksheet.** Record details about each of your assignments, such as the due date, topic, length, and form. The worksheet will also remind you of the stages of the writing process: explore, organize, and write. A blank Writing Process Worksheet for you to photocopy for assignments appears on page xx, and a printable copy is on your Student Companion Site.

7. **Be positive.** All the elements you record in your Self-Evaluation Chart probably are covered in *At a Glance: Paragraphs.* The table of contents, the index, and the Correction Chart on the inside back cover of the book will direct you to the additional instruction you decide you need.

Finally, don't compare yourself with others. Compare yourself with yourself and, as you make progress, consider yourself what you are—a student on the path toward effective writing, a student on the path toward success.

Writing Process Worksheet

Title _____

Name _____ Due Date _____

Assignment   In the space below, write whatever you need to know about your assignment, including information about the topic, audience, pattern of writing, length, whether to include a rough draft or revised drafts, and whether your paper must be typed.

Stage One   **Explore**   Freewrite, brainstorm (list), cluster, or take notes as directed by your instructor. Use separate paper if you need more space.

Stage Two   **Organize**   Write a topic sentence or thesis; label the subject and focus parts.

Write an outline or a structured list. For reading-based writing, include quotations and references with page numbers.

Stage Three   **Write**   On separate paper, write and then revise your paragraph or essay as many times as necessary for **c**oherence, **l**anguage (usage, tone, and diction), **u**nity, **e**mphasis, **s**upport, and **s**entences (**CLUESS**). Read your work aloud to hear and correct any grammatical errors or awkward-sounding sentences.

Edit any problems in fundamentals, such as **c**apitalization, **o**missions, **p**unctuation, and **s**pelling (**COPS**).

1

The Paragraph
and Prewriting

～ The Paragraph Defined

Defining the word *paragraph* requires a bit of thought because there are different kinds of paragraphs, each one having a different purpose within an essay:

Introductory: Usually the first paragraph in an essay, the introductory paragraph gives the necessary background and indicates the main idea, called the **thesis**.

Developmental: A unit of several sentences, the developmental paragraph expands on an idea. This book features the writing of the developmental paragraph. When written by itself, as it frequently is for college writing assignments and tests, the developmental paragraph often resembles a miniature essay in structure.

Transitional: Usually a brief paragraph of one or two sentences, the transitional paragraph merely directs the reader from one point in an essay to another.

Concluding: Usually the last paragraph in an essay, the concluding paragraph makes the final comment on the topic.

Typically, paragraphs written as college assignments are easy to identify because they are indented. Each one starts with skipped spaces at the beginning of the first line. The developmental paragraph featured in this book contains three parts: the subject, the topic sentence, and the support.

The **subject** is what you will write about. At the outset, the subject is likely to be broad or general, and, therefore, must be focused. The **topic sentence** includes both the subject and the focus of that subject. The focus indicates what you plan to *do* with the subject.

1

The topic sentence contains the central, or main, idea of the paragraph. Everything else in the paragraph supports the topic sentence; that is, all the other sentences explain or say more about the central idea. The **support** is the evidence or reasoning that explains the topic sentence. That support can be developed according to several basic patterns. Each pattern is the subject of one chapter of this book. The following questions can help you choose an appropriate pattern or a combination of patterns for your paragraph.

> *Narration:* Can you illustrate your point by telling a story?
>
> *Description:* How does something look, sound, feel, taste, or smell?
>
> *Exemplification:* Can you support your main idea with examples of what you mean?
>
> *Analysis by division:* What are the parts of a unit, and how do they work together?
>
> *Process analysis:* How do you do something? How is (was) something done?
>
> *Cause and effect:* What are the reasons for or the results of an event, a trend, or a circumstance?
>
> *Comparison and contrast*: How are two or more subjects similar and different?
>
> *Definition:* What does a term mean?
>
> *Argument:* What evidence and reasoning will convince someone that you are right?

These patterns are usually combined in writing paragraphs and essays, though one pattern will often provide the overreaching structure. Regardless of the pattern or combination you use, the definition of the developmental paragraph remains the same. A **developmental paragraph** is a group of sentences, each with the function of supporting a single main idea, which is contained in the topic sentence. Here is a brief example by a professional writer:

> A cat's tail is a good barometer of its intentions. An excited or aggressively aroused cat will whip its entire tail back and forth. When I talk to Sam, he holds up his end of the conversation by occasionally flicking the tip of his tail. Mother cats move their tails back and forth to invite their kittens to play. A kitten raises its tail perpendicularly to beg for attention; older cats may do so to beg for food. When your cat holds its tail aloft while crisscrossing in front of you, it is trying to say, "Follow me"—usually to the kitchen, or more precisely, to the

refrigerator. Unfortunately, many cats have lost their tails in refrigerator doors as a consequence.

–Michael W. Fox, "What Is Your Pet Trying to Tell You?"

The paragraph begins with the topic sentence: "A cat's tail is a good barometer of its intentions." The other sentences provide support for the topic sentence; they give examples to show that the topic sentence is credible. The final sentence adds humor to the writing and gives a sense of ending, or closure.

Although the topic sentence is often the first sentence of the paragraph, it does not have to be. Furthermore, the topic sentence is sometimes restated or echoed at the end of the paragraph, although again it does not have to be. However, a well-phrased concluding sentence can emphasize the central idea of the paragraph as well as provide a nice balance and ending.

A paragraph is not a constraining formula; in fact, it has variations. In some instances, for example, the topic sentence is not found in a single sentence. It may be the combination of two sentences, or it may be an easily understood but unwritten underlying idea that unifies the paragraph. Nevertheless, the paragraph in most college writing contains discussion supporting a stated topic sentence, and the instruction in this book is based on that fundamental idea.

⌒ A Sample Paragraph

The following paragraph was written by college student Cyrus Norton. The topic sentence, including the subject of the paragraph and the focus of the paragraph, have been underlined. Norton's topic sentence (not the first sentence in this instance), his support of the topic sentence, and his concluding sentence have been identified in the margin.

This is the final draft. Following it, we will back up and, in this chapter and the next, show how Norton moved during the writing process from his initial idea to this final paragraph.

```
        Magic Johnson, an NBA Great
               Cyrus Norton


      Some NBA (National Basketball
   Association) players are good because they
   have a special talent in one area. Magic
```

Topic sentence — Johnson was a great NBA star because he was excellent in shooting, passing, rebounding,

Support for shooting — and leading. As a shooter, few have ever equaled him. He could slam, shovel, hook, and fire from three-point range—all with deadly accuracy. As for free throws, he led all NBA players in shooting percentage in 1988-89. While averaging more than twenty points per

Support for passing — game, he helped others become stars with his passes. As the point guard (the quarterback of basketball), he was always near the top in the league in assists and was famous for his "no-look" pass, which often surprised even his teammates with its precision. When he wasn't shooting or passing, he was

Support for rebounding — rebounding. A top rebounding guard is unusual in professional basketball, but Magic, at six feet, nine inches, could bump shoulders and leap with anyone. These three qualities made him probably the most spectacular triple-double threat of all time. "Triple-double" means reaching two digits in scoring, assists, and rebounding. Magic didn't need more for greatness in the NBA, but he had more. With his everlasting smile and

Support for leading — boundless energy, he was also an inspirational team leader. He always believed in himself and his team. When his team was down by a point and three seconds remained on the game clock, the fans looked for Magic to get the ball. They watched as he dribbled once, he faded, he leaped, he twisted, and he

Concluding sentence — hooked one in from twenty feet! That was magic. That was Magic.

Let's consider Norton's paragraph in the light of what we know about paragraphs in general. Magic Johnson, the subject, is what the paragraph is all about. In this example, the title also names the subject. The topic sentence, the unifying and controlling idea, makes a clear statement about what the writer will say about the subject. As usual, the topic sentence appears near the beginning of the paragraph. The support gives evidence and examples to back up the controlling idea. The last sentence, "That was Magic," echoes the topic sentence. It is usually called the concluding sentence.

The author has told you what he was going to say, he has said it, and finally he has reminded you of what he has told you. The concluding sentence is sometimes omitted. The two most common designs of developmental paragraphs in college writing are these:

> Topic sentence→support→concluding sentence
> Topic sentence→support

"Magic Johnson, an NBA Great" is a typical paragraph: a group of sentences that present and develop an idea. In college writing, a paragraph is usually expository; that is, its purpose is to explain. In this example, you, the reader, get the point. You're informed, and maybe even entertained, by the explanation.

If you follow certain principles and then practice, practice, practice, you too can write effective paragraphs. Success lies in following directions and using the right set of tools.

Principles at a Glance

Paragraph:	A group of sentences that present and develop an idea.
Topic sentence:	The sentence that expresses the controlling idea of the paragraph. The topic sentence mentions the subject (what the paragraph is about) and the treatment (what the writer will say about the subject).
Support:	Evidence such as details, examples, and explanations that explain the topic sentence.
Basic paragraph designs:	Topic sentence→support→concluding sentence Topic sentence→support

The Writing Process

Writing does not mean merely putting words on paper. It is a process that often involves several steps: using prewriting techniques to explore a topic, limiting and then developing the topic, making an outline, writing a draft, revising the draft as many times as necessary, and editing. Writers sometimes discover that their topic sentence or their outline does not work, and they go back and alter their original concept or design.

For flexible, systematic guidance, consider the Writing Process Worksheet on page xx. It can be copied, enlarged, and submitted with your assignment, if your instructor asks you to do so. It also can be printed from the Student Companion Site.

Prewriting: Using the Blank Sheet of Opportunity

Certain strategies commonly grouped under the heading *prewriting* can help you get started and develop your ideas. Actually, these strategies—freewriting, brainstorming, clustering, defining a topic, and outlining—are very much a part of writing. The understandable desire to skip to the finished statement is what causes the most common student-writer grief: that of not filling the blank sheet or of filling it but not significantly improving on the void. The prewriting strategies that follow will help you attack the blank sheet constructively with imaginative thought, analysis, and experimentation. They can lead to clear, effective communication.

Although the strategies can work very well, you do not need to use all of them in all writing assignments. Learn them now, and use them when they are needed. Think of this approach as carrying a box of tools and then selecting the best tools for the job.

Freewriting

Freewriting is an exercise that its originator, Peter Elbow, has called "babbling in print." In freewriting, you write without stopping, letting your ideas tumble forth. You do not concern yourself with the fundamentals of writing, such as punctuation and spelling. Freewriting is an adventure into your memory and imagination. It is concerned with discovery, invention, and exploration. If you are at a loss for words on your subject, write in a comment such as "I don't know what is coming next" or "blah, blah, blah," and continue when relevant words come. It is important to keep writing. Freewriting immediately eliminates the blank page and thereby helps you break through an emotional barrier, but that is not the only benefit. The words that you sort through in that idea kit will include some you can use. You can then underline or circle those words and even add notes on the side so that the freewriting continues to grow even after its initial spontaneous expression.

The way you proceed depends on the type of assignment: working with a topic of your choice, working from a restricted list of topics, or working with a prescribed topic.

Working with the *topic of your choice* affords you the greatest freedom of exploration. You would probably select a subject that interests you and freewrite about it, allowing your mind to wander among its many parts, perhaps mixing fact and fantasy, direct experience, and hearsay. A freewriting about music might uncover areas of special interest and knowledge, such as jazz or folk rock, that you would want to pursue further in freewriting or other prewriting strategies.

Working from a *restricted list* requires a more focused freewriting. With the list, you can, of course, experiment with several topics to discover what is most suitable for you. If, for example, "career choice," "career preparation," "career guidance," and "career prospects" are on the restricted list, you would probably select one and freewrite about it. If it works well for you, you would probably proceed with the next step of your prewriting. If you are not satisfied with what you uncover in freewriting, you would explore another item from the restricted list.

When working with a *prescribed topic*, you focus on a particular topic and try to restrict your freewriting to its boundaries. If your topic specifies a division of a subject area such as "political involvement of your generation," then you would tie those key words to your own information, critical thinking, and imaginative responses. If the topic is restricted to, say, your reaction to a particular reading selection such as a poem, then that poem would give you the framework for your free associations with your own experiences, creations, and opinions.

You should learn to use freewriting because it will often serve you well, but you need not use it every time you write. Some very short writing assignments do not call for freewriting. An in-class assignment may not allow time for freewriting.

Nevertheless, freewriting is often a useful strategy in your toolbox of writing techniques. It can help you get words on paper, break emotional barriers, generate topics, develop new insights, and explore ideas.

Freewriting can lead to other stages of prewriting and writing, and it can also provide content as you develop your topic.

The following example of freewriting, and the writing, revising, and editing examples in Chapter 2, are from student Cyrus Norton's paragraph, "Magic Johnson, an NBA Great" (p. 3). Norton's topic came from a restricted list; he was directed to write about the success of an individual. Had he been working with a prescribed topic, he might have been directed to concentrate on a specific aspect of Johnson's career, such as business, philanthropy, public service, or the one Norton chose: great basketball playing.

Sample Freewriting

<table>
<tr><td>great</td><td>Magic Johnson was the <u>greatest</u> player I've ever seen in professional basketball.</td></tr>
<tr><td>leader
inspiration</td><td>Actually not just a player but a <u>leader</u> and an <u>inspiration</u> to the team so they always gave him the ball when the game was on the line. It was too bad his career was cut short when they discovered he was HIV positive. Actually he came back but then retired again.</td></tr>
<tr><td>rich</td><td>He made <u>a lot of money</u> and I guess he invested it wisely because his name is linked to the Lakers and theaters and more. Also to programs making people aware of the danger of AIDS and helping kids grow up and stay out of trouble. But the main thing about Magic is</td></tr>
<tr><td>playing</td><td>the <u>way he played</u>. He could do everything. He even played center one time in a championship</td></tr>
<tr><td>scoring</td><td>game. He always <u>scored a lot</u> and he could</td></tr>
<tr><td>passing
rebounding</td><td><u>pass</u> like nobody else. Even though he was a guard, he was tall and could <u>rebound</u>. He was great. Everyone says so.</td></tr>
</table>

After doing this freewriting, Cyrus Norton went back through his work looking for ideas to develop for a writing assignment. As he recognized those ideas, he underlined key words and phrases and made a few notes in the margins. By reading only the underlined words, you can obtain a basic understanding of what is important to him. It is not necessary to underline entire sentences.

In addition to putting some words on that dreaded blank sheet of paper, Norton discovered that he had quite a lot of information about Magic Johnson and that he had selected a favorable topic to develop. The entire process took little time. Had he found few or no promising ideas, he might have freewritten about another topic. In going back through his work, he saw some errors in writing, but he did not correct them because the purpose of freewriting is discovery, not correct grammar, punctuation, or spelling. He was confident that he could then continue with the process of writing a paper.

Brainstorming

Brainstorming features key words and phrases that relate in various ways to the subject area or to the specific topic you are concerned with. One effective way to get started is to ask the big six questions about your subject area: *Who? What? Where? When? Why?* and *How?* Then let your mind run free as you jot down answers in single entries or lists. Some of the big six questions may not fit, and some may be more important than others, depending on the purposes of your writing. For example, if you were writing about the causes of a situation, the *Why?* question could be more important than the others; if you were concerned with how to do something, the *How?* question would predominate. If you were writing in response to a reading selection, you would confine your thinking to questions appropriately related to the content of that reading selection.

Whatever your focus for the questions is, the result is likely to be numerous ideas that will provide information for continued exploration and development of your topic. Thus your pool of information for writing widens and deepens.

An alternative to asking the big six questions is simply to make a list of words and phrases related to your subject area or specific topic. That technique, favored by many professional writers and scholars, is called **listing**.

Cyrus Norton continued with the topic of Magic Johnson and he tightened his topic to focus on particular areas. Although Norton could have listed the annotations and the words he underlined in his freewriting, he used the big six questions for his framework.

Who?	Magic Johnson
What?	great basketball player
Where?	the NBA
When?	for more than ten years
Why?	love of game and great talent
How?	shooting, passing, rebounding, leading, coolness, inspiring

As it turned out, *How?* was the most fruitful question for Norton, and it led him to a list.

Clustering

Clustering (also called **mapping**) is yet another prewriting technique. Start by double-bubbling your topic; that is, write it down in the middle of the page and draw a double circle around it. Then respond to the question "What comes to mind?" Single-bubble other ideas on spokes radiating from the hub that contains the topic. Any bubble can lead to another bubble or numerous bubbles in the same way. This strategy is sometimes used instead of or before making an outline to organize and develop ideas.

The more specific the topic inside the double bubble, the fewer the number of spokes that will radiate with single bubbles. For example, a topic such as "high school dropouts" would have more spokes than "reasons for dropping out of high school."

Here is Cyrus Norton's cluster on the subject of Magic Johnson.

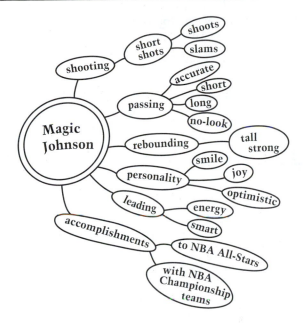

～ Writing the Topic Sentence

The topic sentence is the most important sentence in your prewriting and also in your paragraph. It includes two parts: the subject and the focus (what you will do with your subject). Consider, for example, this topic sentence:

Magic Johnson was a great all-around NBA player.
subject   focus

It is an effective topic sentence because it limits the subject and indicates focus that can be developed in additional sentences. Another sound version is the following, which goes further to include divisions for the focus.

Magic Johnson was a great NBA star because he was excellent
subject   focus

in shooting, passing, rebounding, and leading.

Ineffective topic sentences are often too broad, vague, or too narrow.

VAGUE OR   Magic Johnson was everything to everybody.
TOO BROAD   Magic Johnson was fun.

Magic Johnson was a success in basketball.

Too narrow   Magic Johnson went to Michigan State University.

Magic Johnson signed with the Los Angeles Lakers.

Usually, simple statements of fact do not need or do not allow for development.

Exercise 1 Evaluating Topic Sentences

Mark the following statements for subject (S) and focus (F), and label each as effective (E) or ineffective (I). Effective statements are those that you can easily relate to supporting evidence. Ineffective statements are vague, too broad, or too narrow.

_____   1. Columbus is located in Ohio.

_____   2. Columbus is a fabulous city.

_____   3. Columbus has dealt thoroughly with its housing problems.

_____   4. A monkey is a primate.

_____   5. Monkeys are fun.

_____   6. In clinical studies, monkeys have demonstrated a remarkable ability to reason.

_____   7. More than a million cats are born in California each year.

_____   8. A simple observation of a domesticated cat in the pursuit of game will show that it has not lost its instinct for survival.

_____   9. The two teams in the Rose Bowl have similar records.

_____   10. Michigan State is in the Rose Bowl.

Exercise 2 Writing Topic Sentences

Complete the following entries by making each into a solid topic sentence. Only a subject and part of the focus are provided. The missing part may be more than a single word.

EXAMPLE: Car salespersons behave differently depending on <u>the car</u>
<u>they are selling and the kind of customer they are serving</u>.

1. Television commercials are often _____.

2. Rap music promotes _____.

3. My part-time job taught me _____.

4. I promote environmental conservation by _____.

5. The clothing that a person wears often suggests _____.

6. My close friend is preoccupied with _____.

7. Winning a lot of money is not always _____.

8. Country music appeals to our most basic _____.

9. Friendship depends on _____.

10. A good salesperson should _____.

Exercise 3 Writing Topic Sentences

Write a topic sentence for each of the following subjects.

1. Computer literacy _____.

2. My taste in music _____.

3. Bus transportation _____.

4. The fear of crime _____.

5. An excellent boss _____.

6. Doing well in college English classes_____.

7. Violence on television _____.

8. Child-care centers_____.

9. Good health _____.

10. Teenage voters _____.

⁀ Writing the Outline

An **outline** is a pattern for showing the relationship of ideas. The two main outline forms are the **sentence outline** (each entry is a complete sentence) and the **topic outline** (each entry is a key word or phrase). The topic outline is commonly used for both paragraphs and essays.

Indentation, number and letter sequences, punctuation, and the placement of words are important to clear communication in an outline. We do not read an outline expecting to be surprised by form and content, as we do a poem. We go to the outline for information, and we expect to find ideas easily. Unconventional marks (circles, squares, half-parentheses) and items out of order are distracting and, therefore, undesirable in an outline. The standard form is as easily mastered as a nonstandard form, and it is worth your time to learn it. Outlining is not difficult: the pattern is flexible and can have any number of levels and parts.

Basically, an outline shows how a topic sentence is supported. Thus it shows the organization of the paragraph. The most important supporting material, called the **major support**, is indicated by Roman numerals. That major support is developed by less important supporting material, called the **minor support**, which in turn may be developed by details or examples. Here is the outline developed by Cyrus Norton:

Magic Johnson was a great NBA star because he was excellent in shooting, passing, rebounding, and leading.

I. Shooting (major support)
   A. Short shots (minor support)
      1. Shovel (detail)
      2. Slam-dunk (detail)
   B. Long shots (minor support)
   C. Free throws (minor support)

II. Passing (major support)
   A. No-look (minor support)
   B. Precise (minor support)
III. Rebounding (major support)
   A. Leaping (minor support)
   B. Bumping shoulders (minor support)
IV. Leading (major support)
   A. Energy (minor support)
   B. Spirit (minor support)
      1. Faith (detail)
      2. Smile (detail)

The foundation of a good outline and hence a good paragraph is a strong topic sentence, which means one with a specific subject and a well-defined focus. After writing a good topic sentence, the next step is to divide the focus into parts. Just what the parts are will depend on what you specify in the focus. Consider the thought process involved. What sections of material would be appropriate in your discussion to support or explain that topic sentence?

Among the most common forms of division are the following:

- Divisions of time or incident to tell a story

    I. Situation
   II. Conflict
  III. Struggle
  IV. Outcome
   V. Meaning

- Divisions of examples or divisions of one example into three or more aspects

    I. First example (aspect)
   II. Second example (aspect)
  III. Third example (aspect)

- Divisions of causes or effects

    I. Cause (or effect) one
   II. Cause (or effect) two
  III. Cause (or effect) three

- Divisions of a unit into parts (such as the federal government into executive, legislative, and judicial branches—or Magic Johnson's all-around skill into shooting, passing, rebounding, and leading)

    I. Part one
   II. Part two
  III. Part three

- Divisions of how to do something or how something was done

    I. Preparation
   II. Steps
      A. Step 1
      B. Step 2
      C. Step 3

Exercise 4 Completing Basic Outline Patterns

Fill in the missing outline parts. Consider whether you are dealing with time, examples, causes, effects, parts, or steps. Answers will vary, depending on individual experiences and views.

1. Too many of us are preoccupied with material things.

    I. Clothing

   II. Cars

  III. _____

2. Television sitcoms may vary, but every successful show has certain components.

    I. Good acting

   II. _____

  III. Good situations

  IV. _____

3. A female who is trying to discourage unwanted sexual advances should take several measures.

    I. _____

   II. Set clear boundaries

  III. Avoid compromising situations

4. Concentrating during reading involves various techniques.

    I. Preview material

    II. Pose questions

    III. _____

5. Crime has some bad effects on a nearby neighborhood.

    I. People fearful

        A. Don't go out at night

        B. _____

    II. People without love for neighborhood

        A. _____

        B. Put houses up for sale

    III. People as victims

        A. Loss of possessions

        B. _____

6. Exercising can improve a person's life.

    I. Looks better

        A. Skin

        B. _____

    II. Feels better

        A. _____

        B. Body

    III. Performs better

        A. Work

        B. _____

7. Shoppers in department stores can be grouped according to needs.

    I. _____

    II. Special-needs shoppers

    III. Bargain hunters

8. There are different kinds of intelligence based on situations.

   I. Street-smart

   II. Common sense

   III. _____

9. Smoking should be discouraged.

   I. Harm to smokers

      A. _____

      B. Cancer risk

   II. Harm to those around smokers

      A. _____

      B. Fellow workers

   III. Cost

      A. Industry—production and absenteeism

      B. _____

10. An excellent police officer must have six qualities.

   I. _____

   II. Knowledge of law

   III. _____

   IV. Emotional soundness

   V. Skill in using weapons

   VI. _____

Writer's Guidelines at a Glance:
The Paragraph and Prewriting

1. A **paragraph** is a group of sentences, each with the function of stating or supporting a single controlling idea that is contained in the topic sentence.
2. A paragraph contains two parts: the topic sentence and the support.

- The topic sentence expresses the controlling idea of the paragraph. It has a subject (what the paragraph is about) and a focus (what the writer will do with the subject).
- The support is the evidence (details, examples, and explanations) that backs up the topic sentence.

3. The two most common paragraph designs in college writing are these:

- Topic sentence→support→concluding sentence
- Topic sentence→support

4. Prewriting includes activities you do before writing your first draft or whenever you need new ideas.

- **Freewriting:** writing without stopping, letting your ideas tumble forth. Freewriting helps you break emotional barriers, generate topics, and discover and explore ideas.
- **Brainstorming:** a listing procedure that helps you discover key words and phrases that relate to your topic. Simply make a list, or ask *Who? What? Where? When? Why?* and *How?* questions of your topic.
- **Clustering:** a graphic way of showing connections and relationships. Start by double-bubbling your topic. Then ask "What comes to mind?" and single-bubble other ideas on spokes radiating from the double bubble.

5. The **topic sentence** includes the subject (what you are writing about) and focus (what you are doing with your subject).

6. The **outline** is a form for indicating the relationship of ideas. An outline shows how a topic sentence is supported. Thus it reveals the organization of the paragraph. Major support is indicated by Roman numerals. The major support is developed by minor support, which in turn may be developed by details or examples.

Topic sentence
I. Major support
   A. Minor support
   B. Minor support
      1. Details or examples
      2. Details or examples
II. Major support
   A. Minor support
   B. Minor support

2

Writing, Revising,
and Editing the Paragraph

〜 Writing Your First Draft

Once you have completed your topic sentence and outline (or list or cluster), you are ready to begin writing your paragraph. The initial writing is called the **first**, or **rough**, **draft**. Your topic sentence is likely to be at or near the beginning of your paragraph and will be followed by your support as ordered by your outline.

Paying close attention to your outline for basic organization, you should proceed without worrying about the refinements of writing. This is not the time to concern yourself with perfect spelling, grammar, or punctuation. After you have finished that first draft, take a close look at it. If your topic sentence is sound and your outline has served you well, you have a basic discussion. You have made a statement and supported it, and you are on your way to writing a good paragraph.

Don't be embarrassed by the roughness of your work. You should be embarrassed only if you leave it that way. You are seeing the reason why a first draft is called "rough." Famous authors have said publicly that they wouldn't show their rough drafts even to their closest, most forgiving friends.

The Recursive Factor

The process of writing can be called **recursive**, which means "going back and forth." In this respect, writing is like reading. If you do not understand what you have read, you back up and read it again. After you have reread a passage, you may still need to read selectively. The same can be said of writing. If, for example, after having developed an outline and started writing your first draft, you discover that your subject is too broad, you have to back up, narrow your

20

topic sentence, and then adjust your outline. You may even want to return to an early list or cluster of ideas to see how you can use a smaller grouping of them. Revision is usually the most recursive of all parts of the writing process. You will go over your material again and again until you are satisfied that you have expressed yourself as well as you possibly can.

Revising Your Writing

The term *first draft* suggests quite accurately that there will be other drafts, or versions, of your writing. Only in the most dire situations, such as an in-class examination when you have time for only one draft, should you be satisfied with a single effort.

What you do beyond the first draft is revising and editing. Revision is concerned with organization, content, and language effectiveness. Editing involves a final correcting of mistakes in spelling, punctuation, and capitalization. In practice, editing and revision are not always separate activities, although writers usually wait until the next-to-the-last draft to edit some minor details and attend to other small points that can be easily overlooked.

Successful revision almost always involves intense, systematic rewriting. You should learn to look for certain aspects of skillful writing as you enrich and repair your first draft. To help you recall these aspects so that you can keep them in mind and examine your material comprehensively, this textbook offers a memory device—an acronym in which each letter suggests an important feature of good writing and revision. This device enables you to memorize the features of good writing quickly. Soon you will be able to recall the features and refer to them automatically. These features need not be attended to individually when you revise your writing, although they may be. And they need not be attended to in the order presented here. The acronym is CLUESS (pronounced "clues"), which provides this guide:

*C*oherence
*L*anguage
*U*nity
*E*mphasis
*S*upport
*S*entences

Coherence

Coherence is the flow of ideas, with each idea leading logically and smoothly to the next. It is achieved by numbering parts or otherwise indicating time (*first, second, third, then, next, soon,* and so on), giving directions (according to space, as in "To the right is a map, and to the left of that map is a bulletin board"), using transitional words (*however, otherwise, therefore, similarly, hence, on the other hand, then, consequently, accordingly, thus*), using demonstrative pronouns (*this, that, those*), and moving in a clear order (from the least important to the most important or from the most important to the least important).

Language

Language here means using words that are suitable for what you are writing and for your audience. In college writing that means you will usually avoid slang and clichés such as "a barrel of laughs," "happy as a clam," and "six of one and a half dozen of another." Your writing will contain standard grammar and usage. Effective writing also includes words that will convey your ideas with precision. Avoid general words such as "transportation" when a specific one such as "bus" would serve you better. Also avoid abstract words such as "cool" when a concrete word or phrase such as "faded jeans" would make your meaning clear.

Unity

Unity begins with a good topic sentence. Everything in your paragraph should be related and subordinated to your topic sentence. Repetition of a key word or phrase can make the unity even stronger.

Emphasis

Emphasize, or stress, important ideas by using **position** (the most emphatic parts of a work are the beginning and the end), **repetition** (repeat key words and phrases), and **isolation** (a short, direct sentence among longer ones will usually command attention).

Support

Support is the material that backs up, justifies, or proves your topic sentence. Work carefully with the material from your outline (or list or cluster) to make sure that your ideas are well supported. If your paragraph is skimpy and your ideas slender, you are probably generalizing and not explaining how you arrived at your conclusions. Avoid repetition that does not add to the content; use details and examples; indicate parts and discuss relationships; and explain why your generalizations are true, logical, and accurate. Your readers can't accept your ideas unless they know by what reasoning or use of evidence you developed them.

Sentences

Be sure your **sentences** are complete (not fragments) and that you have not incorrectly combined word groups that should be sentences (comma splices and run-ons). Consider using different types of sentences and different sentence beginnings. (See Chapter 14, pages 183–189.)

Write as many drafts as necessary, revising as you go for all the aspects of effective writing. Don't confuse revising with editing (the final stage of the writing process); don't get bogged down in fixing such things as spelling and punctuation.

⌒ Adding Editing to Your Revision

Editing, the final stage of the writing process, involves a careful examination of your work. Look for problems with capitalization, omissions, punctuation, and spelling (COPS).

Before you submit your writing to your instructor, do what almost all professional writers do before sending their material along: Read it aloud, to yourself or to a willing accomplice. Reading material aloud will help you catch any awkwardness of expression, omission and misplacement of words, and other problems that are easily overlooked by an author.

As you can see, writing is a process and is not a matter of just sitting down and "banging out" a statement. The parts of the process from prewriting to revising to editing are connected, and your movement is ultimately forward, but this process allows you to go back and forth in the recursive manner discussed earlier. If your outline is not working, perhaps the flaw is in your topic sentence. You may need to go back and fix it. If one section of your paragraph is skimpy, perhaps you will have to go back and reconsider the pertinent material in your outline or cluster. There you might find more details or alter a statement so that you can move into more fertile areas of thought.

Cyrus Norton wrote this first draft, marked it for revision, and then completed the final draft, which you read on pages 3–4. For simplification, only this draft is shown, although a typical paper might require several drafts, including one on which the author has done nothing but edit his or her revised writing.

Magic Johnson ^, ^ an NBA Great

(National Basketball Association)
Some NBA ^ players are good because they
have a special talent
^ ~~are good~~ in one area ^. ~~such as shooting,~~
~~passing, or rebounding.~~ Magic Johnson was ^ a
NBA star | excellent | shooting, passing,
great ^ because he was ^ ~~good~~ in ^ ~~all of those~~
rebounding, and leading
~~things and more~~. As a shooter few have ~~been~~
ever equaled him
^ ~~able to do what he could~~. He could slam,
shovel, hook, and fire from three-point
—all with deadly accuracy | As for
ran/ge ^. ~~When it came to~~ ^ free throws, he led
all NBA players in shooting percentage in
While
1988-89. ~~Then~~ ^ he averaged more than twenty
points per game, he helped others become
with his passes | (the quarterback of basketball) ^,
stars ^. As the point guard ^ he was always near
s
the top in the league in a ^ sists and was
famous for his ^ " no ^ - look ^ " passe~~d~~ ^, ~~W~~hich often
its
surprised even his teammates with ^ ~~their~~
When he wasn't shooting or passing, he was rebounding.
precision. ^ A top rebounding guard is unusual,
but Magic, ~~standing~~ at six feet nine inches
u
tall, could bump sho ^ lders and jump with

anyone. These three qualities made him

probably the most spectacular triple-double

"Triple-double" means reaching two digits in scoring, assists, and rebounding.
threat of all time. Magic didn't need more
                   ∧

for greatness in the NBA, but he had more. He
                                        ∧

was also an inspirational team leader with
≡

his everlasting smile and boundless energy.
                                         ∧

He   ed
∧Always believ~~ing~~ in himself and his team.
∧   ∧

When his team was down by a point and three

remained on the game clock   the fans
seconds ~~were left~~, ~~you~~ always looked for
        ∧   ∧

                                      They
Magic to get the ball. ~~Then you~~ watched as he
                                   ∧

             he   he   he
dribbled once, faded, leaped, twisted, and
              ∧   ∧   ∧

he   !   That was magic.
∧hooked one in from twenty feet That was
∧   ∧∧

Magic.

Exercise 1 Revising and Editing

*Treat the following paragraph as your own rough draft, and mark it in the way Cyrus Norton marked his rough draft. First consider **c**oherence, **l**anguage, **u**nity, **e**mphasis, **s**upport, and **s**entences (**CLUESS**). Then edit the paragraph, correcting fundamentals such as **c**apitalization, **o**missions, **p**unctuation, and **s**pelling (**COPS**).*

Delete Dress Codes

High school dress codes don't make any sense to me.

I've heard all the reasons. Too many kids wear gang clothes

and some get attacked or even killed. Parents have to put

up too much money and even then the kids without parents
with deep pockets can't compete. And then there are those
that say kids behave bad if they dress in a free spirit
way. Let's take them one at a time. As for the gang stuff,
it's mainly how you act, not how you look, and if the gang
stuff is still a problem, then just ban certain items of
clothing. You don't have to go to the extreames of
uniforms, just change the attitude, not the clothes. Then
comes the money angle. Let the kid get a part-time job if
they want better clothes. The behavior number is not what
I can relate to. I mean, you go to class and learn, and you
do it the school way, but the way you dress should have
something to do with how you want to express yourself. Do
they want to turn out a bunch of little robots that think
the same way, behave the same way, and yes with the dress
code even look the same way. Get real! If they'll cut us
some slack with how we dress, they'll get happier campers
in the classroom. Later better-citizens in society.

Exercise 2 Revising and Editing

*Revise the following student first draft. Then check for **c**apitalization, **o**missions (oversights or grammar problems), **p**unctuation, and **s**pelling (**COPS**). Space is provided for you to add, delete, move, and correct material.*

Pain Unforgettable

One evening in 2008 while I was working the swing
shift at the General Tire Recapping Plant. I came up with
the greatest pain of my life because of a terible

accident. Raw rubber was heated up in a large tank. Pryor to its being fed into an extruder. I was recapping large off-road tires. The lowering platform was in the up position the chain snapped. It sent the heavy platform crashing down into the tank. This caused a huge wave of steaming water to surge out of the tank. Unfortunately, I was in its path the wave hit my back just above my waist. The sudden pain shook me up. I could not move. My clothes were steaming I freaked out. Co-workers ran to my aid and striped the hot clothing from my body, taking skin as they did. I lay face down on the plant floor, naked and shaking for a long time. The paramedics came to pick me up. The painful experience is still scary when I think about it.

Exercise 3 Revising and Editing

*Mark the following rough draft for **c**oherence, **l**anguage, **u**nity, em-phasis, **s**upport, and **s**entences (**CLUESS**). Then edit it, correcting fundamentals such as **c**apitalization, **o**missions, **p**unctuation, and spelling (**COPS**).*

If I Were a Traffic Cop

Make me a traffic cop, and I'll crack down on certain types of driver. First off are the drunks. I'd zap them off the highways right off, and any cop would. But what I'm really talking about is the jerks of the highway. Near the top are the up-tight lane changers, for example, this morning when I was driving to school, I saw several. I could have carved at least a couple notches in a vilation pad, and I wasn't even cranky. They cut off

people and force their way in, and leave behind upset and
hurt people. Then there's the left-turn bullies the ones
that keep moving out when the yellow turn to red. They
come in all ages and sexes, they can be young or old,
male or female. Yesterday, I saw this female in a pick-up
barrel right out into the teeth of a red light. She had a
baby on board. She had lead in her foot. She had evil in
her eye. She was hostile and self-centered. Taking
advantage of others. She knew that the facing traffic
would probably not pull out and risk a head-on crash. The
key word there is probably but many times people with a
green light do move out and colide with the left turn
bullies. Third, I'd sap the tailgaters. No one goes fast
enough for these guys. I'm not alone in this peeve. One
bumper sticker reads, "Stay back. I chew tobacky." And
James Bond sprayed oil on cars that chased him. Since the
first is dirty and the second is against the law, if I
had the clout of a Rambo-cop I'd just rack up a lot of
tailgater tickets. But there's a lot of road demons out
there. Maybe it's good I'm not a traffic cop, Rambo or
otherwise, cause traffic cops are suppose to inforce
hundreds of laws. I don't know if I'd have time cause I
have my own pet peeves in mind.

Exercise 4   Writing a Paragraph

Fill in the following two blanks to complete the topic sentence.
_____ *[person's name] is an excellent* _____
[boss, coach, doctor, neighbor, parent, preacher, teacher, sibling].

Then use the topic sentence to write a paragraph. Go through the complete writing process. Use one or more prewriting techniques (freewriting, brainstorming, listing, clustering, outlining), write a first draft, revise your draft as many times as necessary, edit your work, and write a final, polished paragraph.

In your drafts, you may rephrase the topic sentence as necessary. Using the paragraph on pages 3–4 (showing Magic Johnson as a shooter, passer, rebounder, and leader) as a model, divide your topic into whatever qualities make your subject an excellent example of whichever type of person you have chosen.

Writer's Guidelines at a Glance: Writing, Revising, and Editing

1. **Write the rough draft.** Referring to your outline for guidance and to your topic sentence for limits, write a first, or rough, draft. Do not get caught up in correcting and polishing your writing during this stage.
2. **Revise.** Mark and revise your rough draft, rewriting as many times as necessary to produce an effective paragraph. The main points of revision are contained in the acronym CLUESS, expressed here as questions.

   Coherence: Does the material flow smoothly from one idea to the next?

   Language: Are the words appropriate for the message, occasion, and audience?

   Unity: Are all the ideas related to and subordinate to the topic sentence?

   Emphasis: Have you used techniques such as repetition and placement of ideas to emphasize your main point(s)?

   Support: Have you presented material to back up, justify, or prove your topic sentence?

   Sentences: Have you used some variety of structure and avoided fragments, comma splices, and run-ons?

3. **Edit.** Examine your work carefully. Look for problems in capitalization, omissions, punctuation, and spelling (COPS).

3

From Reading
to Writing

∼ Reading-Based Writing

The Writing Component

Reading-based writing was invented to help you easily fill those intimidating blank pages with thoughtful statements centered on what you have read, commonly called the *source*, or *text*. *Text* is a broad term that includes items as diverse as photos, advertisements, online postings, and movies as sources for what is called *text-based writing*, but in this book we are concerned with writing about reading, naturally called *reading-based writing*. For instruction in this book, reading-based writing comes in three forms: summary, reaction, and two-part response. In writing a summary, you use your own words to restate the main ideas in what you have read. In writing a reaction, you comment critically on what you have read, while giving credit for the ideas and words you borrow. Then, in composing a two-part response, you write both a summary and a reaction, but you separate them to show your instructors that you know the difference between the two forms.

The Reading Component

Reading-based writing can also make you a better reader. When you are reading, you concentrate more because you are thinking about how you will be using the reading content in writing. When you are writing, your mind reflects back on what you have read, running ideas critically by your windows of experiences and your banks of knowledge. Reading-based writing represents the complete *you* as a thinking, feeling person in relation to what you have read. In fact, reading-based writing is what we call the essence, or core, of critical thinking.

30

Reading-Based Writing and Other Approaches in Writing

Reading-based writing will serve you well in classrooms across your campus and also in your career. Of course, this book presents a range of writing approaches that may not make use of reading-based writing, including those called *personal experience, individual perspective, cross-curricular, career-related,* and *reading-related.* All of these approaches are presented in this book with instruction, examples, exercises, and suggested topics and prompts. Some approaches overlap, but each has a main thrust with variations imposed by particular writing objectives.

～ Reading Techniques and Reading-Based Writing Forms

Reading-based writing is presented in this early chapter because all writing instruction in this book involves reading in some way. The abundant student and professional readings (more than thirty) were selected to stimulate thought and discussion, to provide content for writing, and to inform writing by strong examples of techniques and forms. Even reading-based writing has its own different forms, and reading itself has its own techniques. Those techniques and forms are shown here in a concise outline of the instruction that covers the remainder of this chapter:

I. Reading techniques
   A. Underlining
   B. Annotating
   C. Outlining
   D. Taking notes
II. Reading-based writing forms
   A. Summary
   B. Reaction
   C. Two-part response

～ Reading Techniques

Underlining

One way to build concentration in reading is to develop a relationship with the reading material. Imagine you are reading a chapter of several pages, and you decide to underline and write in the margins. Immediately, the underlining takes you out of the passive, television-watching frame of mind. You are involved. You are participating. It is now necessary for you to discriminate, to distinguish more important from less important ideas. Perhaps you have thought of underlining as a method designed only to help you with reviewing; that is, when you study the material the next time, you will not have to reread all the material. Instead, you can review only the most important, underlined parts. However, even while you are underlining, you are benefiting from an imposed concentration because this procedure forces you to think, to focus. Consider the following guidelines for underlining:

1. Underline the main ideas in paragraphs. The most important statement, the topic sentence, is likely to be at the beginning of the paragraph.
2. Underline the support for those main ideas.
3. Underline answers to questions that you bring to the reading assignment. These questions may have come from the end of the chapter, from subheadings that you turn into questions, or from your independent concern about the topic.
4. Underline only the key words. You would seldom underline all the words in a sentence and almost never in a whole paragraph.

Does that fit your approach to underlining? Possibly not. Most students, in their enthusiasm to do a good job, overdo underlining.

Maybe you have had this experience: You start reading about something you have not encountered before. The idea seems important. You highlight it. The next idea is equally fresh and significant. You highlight it. A minute or two later, you have changed the color of the page from white to yellow, but you haven't accomplished anything.

The trick is how to figure out what to underline. You would seldom underline more than about 30 percent of a passage, although the amount would depend on your purpose and the nature of the material. Following the preceding four rules will be useful. Learning more about the principles of sentence, paragraph, and essay organization will also be helpful. These principles are presented in Chapters 1 and 2.

Annotating

Annotating, a practice related to underlining, is writing in the margins. You can do it independently, although it usually appears in conjunction with underlining to mark the understanding and to extend the involvement.

Writing in the margins represents intense involvement because it makes the reader a writer. If you read material and write something in the margin as a reaction to it, then in a way you have begun a conversation with the author. The author has made a statement and you have responded. In fact, you may have added something to the text; therefore, for your purposes you have become a coauthor or collaborator. The comments you make in the margin are of your own choosing according to your interests and the purpose you bring to the reading assignment. Your response in the margin may merely echo the author's ideas, it may question them critically, it may relate them to something else, or it may add to them.

In the following example, you can see how the reader has reinforced the underlining by commenting in the margin.

Women and Witchcraft

Mary Beth Norton

Salem witchcraft— broad interest	1 The Salem witchcraft crisis of 1692 to 1693, in which a small number of adolescent girls and young women accused hundreds of older women (and a few men) of having bewitched them, has fascinated Americans ever since. It has provided material for innumerable books, plays, movies, and television productions. To Americans of the twenty-first century the belief in witchcraft in the seventeenth-century colonies is difficult to explain or understand; perhaps that is why the Salem episode has attracted so much attention. For those interested in studying women's experiences, of course, witchcraft incidents are particularly intriguing. The vast majority of suspected witches were female, and so, too,
Why mostly women?	were many of their accusers. Although colonial women rarely played a role on the public stage, in witchcraft cases they were the primary actors. What accounts for their prominence under these peculiar circumstances?
Historical/ cultural background	2 To answer that question, the Salem crisis must be placed into its proper historical and cultural context. People in the early modern world believed in witchcraft because it offered a rationale for events that otherwise seemed random

Without modern science

and unfathomable. In the absence of modern scientific knowledge about such natural phenomena as storms and diseases, and clear explanations for accidents of various sorts, the evil actions of a witch could provide a ready answer to a person or community inquiring about the causes of a disaster.

Witch hunts in Europe— the extent

3   Therefore, witchcraft accusations—and some large-scale witch hunts—were not uncommon in Europe between the early fourteenth and the late seventeenth centuries (1300 to 1700). In short, the immigrants to the colonies came from a culture in which belief in witchcraft was widespread and in which accusations could result in formal prosecutions and executions. Recent research has demonstrated that the Salem incident, although the largest and most important witch hunt in New England, was just one of a number of such episodes in the American colonies.

Question— repeated

Answers: 1
2
3
Women seen as "out of their place"

4   But why were witches women? Admittedly, historians have not yet answered that question entirely satisfactorily. Certain observations can be made: women gave birth to new life and seemed to have the potential to take life away. In Western culture, women were seen as less rational than men, more linked to the natural world, in which magic held sway. Men, who dominated European society, defined the characteristics of a proper woman, who was submissive and accepted a subordinate position. The stereotypical witch, usually described as an aggressive and threatening older woman, represented the antithesis of that image. These broad categories need further refinement, and historians are currently looking closely at the women who were accused of practicing witchcraft to identify the crucial characteristics that set them apart from their contemporaries and made them a target for accusations.

—*Mary Beth Norton*, Major Problems in American Women's History

Exercise 1 Underlining and Annotating

Mark the following paragraphs with underlining and annotation. Compare your marks with those of your classmates.

Buddha Taught Nonviolence

1   Buddha gave his first sermon to the five wisdom seekers who had been his companions. That sermon was a landmark in the history of world religions. Buddha taught the four main ideas that had come to him in his enlightenment, calling them the Four Noble Truths.

2   *First Noble Truth*: Everything in life is suffering and sorrow.

3   *Second Noble Truth*: The cause of all this pain is people's self-centered cravings and desires. People seek pleasure that cannot last and leads only to rebirth and more suffering.

4   *Third Noble Truth*: The way to end all pain is to end all desires.

5   *Fourth Noble Truth*: People can overcome their desires and attain enlightenment by following the Eightfold Path.

6   The Eightfold Path was like a staircase. According to Buddha, those who sought enlightenment had to master one step at a time. The steps of the Eightfold Path were right knowledge, right purpose, right speech, right action, right living, right effort, right mindfulness, and right meditation. By following the Eightfold Path, anyone could attain *nirvana* (nur-VAHN-uh), Buddha's word for release from pain and selfishness.

7   Buddha taught his followers to treat all living things (humans, animals, and even insects) with loving kindness. A devout Buddhist was not even supposed to swat a mosquito.

8   Buddhists and Hindus both sought to escape from the woes of this world, but their paths of escape were very different. Unlike traditional Hinduism, Buddhism did not require complex rituals. Moreover, Buddha taught in everyday language, not in the ancient Sanskrit language of the Vedas and the Upanishads, which most Indians in 500 B.C.E. could no longer understand. Buddha's religion was also unique in its concern for all human beings—women as well as men, lowborn as well as highborn.

Outlining

Outlining can pertain to both reading and writing. Among the writing that will be suggested as assignments in this book are outlines, summaries, and reactions. In some instances, you may use all three forms after reading a passage. The three forms are also associated with reading and critical thinking, in that they contribute to reading comprehension and use systematic and analytical thought. The reading below is followed by student Leon Batista's outline. Note the parallel structure in his outline.

The Roman Toga

1   Practicality has never been a requirement of fashion. The Roman toga was an uncomfortable garment. It was hot in summer, cold in winter, and clumsy for just about any activity but standing still. The toga was, however, practical in one way: It was easy to make, since it involved no sewing. Not even a buttonhole was needed. An adult's toga was basically a large wool blanket measuring about 18 by 7 feet. It was draped around the body in a variety of ways without the use of buttons or pins.

2   In the early days of the Roman republic, both women and men wore togas. Women eventually wore more dresslike garments, called *stolas*, with separate shawls. For men, however, the toga remained in fashion with very little change.

3   Soon after the republic was formed, the toga became a symbol of Roman citizenship. Different styles of togas indicated a male citizen's place in society. For example, a young boy would wear a white toga with a narrow purple band along the border. When his family decided he was ready for adult responsibilities, he would don a pure white toga. On that day, usually when he was about 16, his family would take him to the Forum, where he would register as a full citizen. For the rest of his life, he would wear a toga at the theater, in court, for religious ceremonies, and on any formal occasion. At his funeral his body would be wrapped in a toga to mark him, even in death, as a Roman citizen.

—*Steven L. Jantzen,* World History: Perspectives on the Past

I. Practicality
   A. Not practical
      1. Hot in summer
      2. Cold in winter
      3. Clumsy
   B. Practical
      1. Easy to make
      2. Easy to put on and take off

II. Fashion in Roman republic
   A. Worn by men and women
      1. Changes little with men
      2. Alternates with stolas and shawls for women
   B. Symbol of citizenship
      1. One style for young male
      2. Another style for adult male
         a. Presented at point of adulthood
         b. Worn on all occasions

Taking Notes

Taking notes for reading-based writing in this book should be little more than marking and annotating passages in reading selections and jotting down the useful points for support in your outline as you organize your summary or reaction. While writing, you will use those notes for support as you refer directly to what you have read and you will use some quotations from the reading. You will also give credit to the source you are reading, and—if your instructor requires you to do so—you will use documentation, including page numbers and identification of your source(s) for those ideas and words you borrow.

    Here is an example of how you can place notes inside outlines. It is an excerpt from student Alex Mylonas's reading-based reaction to the short story "The Use of Force" by William Carlos Williams. During his first reading, Alex underlined and annotated freely; then later he selected phrases as support in his outline, which he submitted with a long paragraph assignment.

II. The inner conflict
   A. Doctor versus himself
      1. Wants to be professional
      2. Loses self-control
         "attractive little thing," p. 333
         "damned little brat," p. 333
      3. Loses sight of objective
         "got beyond reason," p. 334
   B. Emotional (brutal) side wins
      "It was a pleasure to attack her," p. 335
      "blind fury," p. 335

〜 Reading-Based Writing Forms

For instruction in this book, reading-based writing comes in three forms: summary, reaction, and two-part response. In writing a summary, you use your own words to restate the main ideas in what you have read. In writing a reaction, you comment critically on what you have read, while giving credit for the ideas and words you borrow. Then, in composing a two-part response, you write both a summary and a reaction, but you separate them to show your instructors that you know the difference between the two forms.

Writing a Summary

A summary is a rewritten, shortened version of a piece of writing in which you use your own wording to express the main ideas. Learning to summarize effectively will help you in many ways. Summary writing reinforces comprehension skills in reading. It requires you to discriminate among the ideas in the target reading passage. A summary is written in the form of a well-designed paragraph. Frequently, summaries are used in collecting material for research papers and in writing conclusions to essays.

The following rules will guide you in writing effective summaries.

1. Cite both the author and the title of the text.
2. Reduce the length of the original by about two-thirds, although the exact reduction will vary depending on the content of the original.
3. Concentrate on the main ideas and include details only infrequently.
4. Change the original wording without changing the idea.
5. Do not evaluate the content or give an opinion in any way (even if you see an error in logic or fact).
6. Do not add ideas (even if you have an abundance of related information).
7. Do not include any personal comments (that is, do not use *I*, referring to self).
8. Use quotations only infrequently. (If you do use quotations, enclose them in quotation marks.)
9. Use author tags ("says York," "according to York," or "the author explains") to remind the reader that you are summarizing the material of another writer.

10. Begin with the main idea (as you usually do in middle paragraphs) and cover the main points in an organized fashion while
using complete sentences.

   The following is a summary of "The Roman Toga," written by
the student who prepared the sample outline. The writing process
used by Batista was direct and systematic. When first reading the
material, he had underlined key parts and written comments and
echo phrases in the margin. Then he wrote his outline. Finally, referring to both the marked passage and the outline, Batista wrote this
summary. Had he not been assigned to write the outline, he might
have done so anyway, as preparation for writing his summary.

Summary of "The Roman Toga"
by Steven L. Jantzen

According to Steven Jantzen in *World
History: Perspectives on the Past*, the toga
was the main form of dress for citizens of
the Roman republic, despite its being "hot in
summer, cold in winter, and clumsy" to wear.
Perhaps the Romans appreciated the simplicity
of wearing a piece of woolen cloth about
eighteen by seven feet "without the use of
buttons or pins." Jantzen explains that the
women also wore another garment similar to a
dress called the *stola*, but Roman male
citizens were likely to wear only the toga—
white with a purple edge for the young and
solid white for the adult. This apparel was
worn from childhood to death.

Exercise 2 Evaluating a Summary

*Compare this summary with the original passage and with the stu-
dent summary you just read. Then mark the instances of poor summary writing by underlining and by using rule numbers from the
preceding list.*

Summary About One of My Favorite Garments

For citizens of the Roman republic, the toga was the main form of dress, despite its being hot in summer, cold in winter, and clumsy to wear. Frankly, I don't see why a bright bunch of people like the Romans couldn't have come up with a better design. Perhaps the Romans appreciated the simplicity of wearing a piece of woolen cloth about eighteen by seven feet without buttons or pins, but I've read elsewhere that the togas were sometimes stolen at the public baths. The women also wore another garment similar to a dress called the *stola*, but the Roman male citizen was likely to wear only the toga—white with a purple edge for the young and solid white for the adult. For the rest of his life, he would wear a toga at the theater, in court, for religious ceremonies, and on any formal occasion. At his funeral, his body would be wrapped in a toga to mark him, even in death, as a Roman citizen.

The following three paragraphs are further examples of reading-based writing: the reaction and the two-part response.

Writing a Reaction

A reaction concentrates on the content in a reading selection or selections. It includes personal experience and other information only to explain, validate, or challenge the ideas in that content.

In the following reaction, student Shanelle Watson takes a basic idea from the original passage and finds historical parallels. She begins and ends her paragraph with references to the content of the reading selection.

Sticks and Stones
Shanelle Watson

Reading "Women and Witchcraft" by Mary
Beth Norton reminded me of a long line of
indignities against women. If something goes
wrong and women can be blamed, they are. For
centuries if a woman did not have babies, it
was said *she* could not, although the man was
just as likely as the woman to be the cause
of her childlessness. If, heaven forbid, the

woman kept having female babies, that woman, it was said, couldn't produce a male. Yet we know now that it is the male who determines the sex of the child. If the child was not bright, as recently as a hundred years ago some doctors said it was because the woman was reading during pregnancy and took away the brain power from the fetus. As a result, many women were not allowed to open a book during pregnancy. Of course, because it was believed that women were so weak, husbands were allowed to beat their wives, but according to English law, the stick could be no thicker than the man's thumb, hence "the rule of thumb." Even voting was argued against by some who said that the typical woman, controlled by emotions, would allow her husband to tell her how to vote, and each married man would then have two votes. It is no wonder that three hundred years ago men looked around and, finding many misfortunes, decided that women were the culprits and should be punished. Sticks were not enough. It was time for stones.

Writing a Two-Part Response

As you have seen, the reaction includes an idea or ideas from a reading or is written with the assumption that readers have read the original piece. However, your instructor may prefer that you separate the forms and present a clear, concise summary followed by another type of reading-based writing. This format is especially useful for critical reactions or problem-solving assignments because it requires you to understand and repeat another's views or experiences before responding. The two-part response also helps you avoid the common problem of writing only a summary of the text when your instructor wants you to both summarize and evaluate or to otherwise react. When writing a summary and a critical reply to a reading assignment, be

sure you know whether your instructor wants you to separate your
summary from your reaction.
    The following reading-based writing first summarizes and then,
in a separate paragraph of reaction, analyzes, evaluates, and inter-
prets the original passage.

"Women and Witchcraft" by Mary Beth Norton:
A Summary and a Reaction
Jeanne Garcia

Part 1: Summary
    Americans have long been fascinated by
the Salem witchcraft plight in 1692 to 1693.
One perplexing factor is that most of the
people accused and many who blamed them were
women. In "Women and Witchcraft," Mary Beth
Norton says the whole issue should be placed
in a historical context. In those times, much
was unknown about the causes of disasters and
illnesses, and the people came to believe
that these things could be attributed to evil
supernatural forces. Consequently, from about
1300 to 1700 "witch hunts" occurred, and
Salem was just one of the locations.
Historians are not certain about why women
were often victims and accusers. They may
have been involved because they had the power
to produce life and, therefore, maybe had
"the potential to take life away." Women were
thought to be more emotional than rational
and even connected to nature, as in magic.
Moreover, the stereotypical witch was
characterized as a mature, assertive woman,
unlike the "proper woman" of the time "who
was submissive and accepted a subordinate
position." Norton says that historians now

seek to discover the precise causes that made
assertive women the victims of persecution as
witches.

Part 2: Reaction

The "witchcraft crisis of 1692 to 1693,"
which Mary Beth Norton discusses in "Women
and Witchcraft," is not so surprising to some
of us who look back after three hundred years
at the way some men treat some women. One
does not have to read between Norton's lines.
She makes it clear that "usually" the people
were "aggressive and threatening older
wom[e]n." The charges came mainly from
adolescent girls and young women, but the
power structure was adult men. Out of
ignorance, the men, often with female
accomplices, were looking around to find
reasons for the misfortunes—bad weather,
diseases, and accidents—that their society
faced. It is a fact that if people are
foolish and desperate enough to look for
witches, they are foolish and desperate
enough to find them. And they did: They found
mainly a few old women who did not know their
place, individuals of a gender associated
with the emotions. If these women had been
meek and mild, if they had been properly
submissive to the menfolk, and if they had
still been young and sexy, they would not
have been vulnerable. But they were what they
were—mature and relatively independent women,
who seemed to be different—and that made them
witches to those who were said not to be
emotionally based—the men.

~ Kinds of Support
for Reading-Based Writing

In your reading-based writing assignments, you are likely to use three methods in developing your ideas: explanations, direct references to the reading selection, and quotations from the reading selection.

- Your explanations will often be expressed in patterns, such as causes and effects, comparison and contrast, definition, or exemplification. These forms are presented in depth and related to reading-based writing in Chapters 5 through 13. Your discussion of personal experience will be used only to explain, validate, or challenge ideas from the reading selection.
- Your references will point your reader(s) directly toward original ideas in sources. The more specific the references, the more helpful they will be to your readers.
- Your quotations will be words borrowed from sources and credited to those sources. You will use quotation marks around those words, which will appear as sentences or as partial sentences blended with your own words.

~ Basic Formal Documentation
in Reading-Based Writing

Borrowing words or ideas without giving credit to the originator is called plagiarism and is not acceptable scholarship, regardless of whether it is intentional. To help you in learning to give credit accurately, your instructor may ask you to document your reading-based writing formally, even though the text is readily available and assigned. Formal documentation means you must indicate the location of all the original ideas you have borrowed, even if you have changed the words.

Citations

Documenting sources for reading-based writing should be done with care. This book uses a system called MLA (Modern Language Association) Style with the 2009 Update. You can find detailed information by keying in "MLA Style 2009" on a search engine such as Google. The *At a Glance* Student Companion Site also has further instructions. Mainly, you need to remember that when using material from a source you must give enough information so that the reader will recognize it or be able to find it in its original context. Here are the most common principles of documentation that can be used for textbook or other restricted sources, whether it is quoted, paraphrased (restated), or summarized.

If you use the author's name in introducing a quotation, then usually give only the page number.

EXAMPLE: Suzanne Britt says that "neat people are bums and clods at heart" (255).

If you use the author's name in introducing a borrowed idea, then usually give only the page number.

EXAMPLE: Suzanne Britt believes that neat people are weak in character (255).

If you do not use the author's name to introduce a quotation or an idea, then usually give both the author's name and the page number.

EXAMPLE: Music often helps Alzheimer's patients think more clearly (Weiss 112).

Works Cited

Work(s) Cited lists the sources used, meaning those that appear in citations, as shown in the previous section. Each kind of publication has its own order of parts and punctuation.

Here is an example of a Work Cited entry pertaining to a student writing. It is "A Work in an Anthology" (covered in the *At a Glance* Companion Site). Note the punctuation between parts and the order of those parts: author's name (last, first), title of composition (quotation marks for a short work; italics for a long work), editor(s) of the anthology, name of the anthology, edition if there is one, place of publication, publisher, date of publication, pages on which the selection appears, and medium of publication.

Work Cited

Ortiz, Charles C. "Not Invulnerable."
     *Sentences, Paragraphs, and Beyond: With
     Integrated Readings*. Ed. Lee Brandon and
     Kelly Brandon. 6th ed. Boston: Cengage,
     2011. 325-26. Print.

∼ Example of Reading-Based Writing

Student Reading-Based Paragraph (extracted from an essay)

Student Lydia Hsiao was asked to read and then write a reading-based reaction to a reading selection taken from Maxine Hong Kingston's The Woman Warrior. *This paragraph taken from Hsiao's short essay illustrates how to document sources.*

Struggling Against Silence

Lydia Hsiao

Maxine Hong Kingston and I came
from a strict Chinese background and were
taught that "a ready tongue is an evil"
(Kingston 252). We were also taught to keep
to ourselves. We were never taught to
communicate with those outside our culture.
This background may have caused my self-
consciousness and my paralyzing fear of being
embarrassed. During my first year in the
United States, I was constantly teased about
my Chinese accent. If I mispronounced a word
during class, I could not help but be
disgusted by my own mistakes, causing me even
greater embarrassment. Kingston says, "[They]
scare the voice away" (254). The result was
that, like Kingston, my potential was for
years undiscovered. In the same way Kingston
allowed silence to "[paint] layers of black
over [her life]" (254), silence continued to
create a thicker darkness in my life. It
first embarrassed me; then it soon robbed me
of my self-esteem. As Kingston says,
"[Talking] takes up that day's courage"
(252). It was almost as if silence was more
than a curtain. It seemed to grow its own

body and walk beside me. That silence became
my sinister friend, taking advantage of my
willingness to accept this cruel school life,
tricking me into believing that home was the
only place I could find my voice. The monster
silence kept me quiet.

Work Cited

Kingston, Maxine Hong. "Silence." *Rereading
    America*. Ed. Gary Colombo, Robert Cullan,
    and Bonnie Lisle. New York: Bedford/
    St. Martin's, 1998. 252-55. Print.

⁓ Essay for Discussion and Writing

The following essay by a student demonstrates many of the elements of good writing that we have been exploring. To help you
evaluate and write in response to the selection, it is underlined
and annotated. It is accompanied by a set of discussion and
critical-thinking questions and then by several reading-based
writing suggestions. Take a look at the questions and writing suggestions before you read the essay to help you focus your reading.

Student Essay

Everyone Pays the Price

Hadley McGraw

*Sitting in a college classroom, Hadley McGraw doesn't remind
one of the stereotypical gang member. Apparently tattoo- and
puncture-free, she is fair-skinned, well-groomed, and soft-spoken.
She does her homework, contributes to class discussion, and
writes well. So much for stereotypes!*

1   It is ten o'clock and time for me to

start my day. I put an X on my calendar to

signify that another twenty-four hours has

passed. I now have one hundred and nine days

until Martin, my boyfriend, comes home. He
has been in jail for the last year. I guess
you could say I was not surprised by his
sentence. This is not the first time, and I
am afraid it will not be the last. Eighteen
months of our three-and-a-half-year
relationship, he has spent in correctional
institutions. Martin is a gang member. He has

Thesis   been a gang member for nine years now. <u>Gang
membership of a loved one affects everyone
around that person.</u> Three-and-a-half years
later I live each day in fear and grief.

Topic 2   <u>I guess what attracted me to Martin at
sentence   first was his bad-boy image and his carefree
way of life.</u> He was good looking and well
known. He was tough and exciting. I, however,
was good and obedient. I had been told often
that I was pretty. I made good grades and
came from a good home. My parents, still
married and drug-free, lived comfortably in a
middle-class neighborhood. Martin, on the

Causes   contrary, <u>came from a broken home. His
parents hated each other. His father was a
cold, heartless man, and his mother was a
"flakey" drug addict. His uncles and cousins
were all members of a very large gang that
"controlled" an area where he lived.</u> Soon he
too was a gang member.

3   Martin quit school when he was a freshman and spent his days on a street corner drinking Olde English forty-ouncers. Soon I was joining him. I began ditching school to hang out. In no time, I was a gang member myself and, as I look back, I see what an

Effects   awful person I became. We used drugs all day and all night. I did not care about anything and neither did he. I left home and devastated my family and lost my friends. I didn't care because I had a new family and new friends. Martin spent his nights committing crimes and dealing drugs. I was by his side, carrying his gun. The drugs made him irritable and violent, and small disagreements turned into huge battles between us. Jail sentences made him angrier and closer to his gang. Each day Martin became farther from me. Life was a nonstop party with his homeboys, and I was his woman. It was exciting and risky. It was self-destructive.

Topic 4   My breaking point was one year ago.
sentence Martin and I were at a party. Everyone was drinking and joking. Oldies were playing and a noisy, wild game of poker was taking place. Suddenly a car was approaching us rapidly. Martin told me to run and hide, so I did.

The homeboys began reaching for their guns.
I heard five gunshots before the car drove
away. I ran to the front of the house where
Martin's cousin lay bleeding. I tried to wake
him, speak to him. He wasn't responding. I
screamed for an ambulance. Finally Martin
appeared from behind a car and ran inside to
call 911. When the ambulance arrived, I was

Effects   hysterical and covered in blood. They took
Martin's cousin to the hospital where he was
pronounced dead. Because of the gunshot
wounds, the funeral was a closed-casket
affair and very hard on everyone. It made
Martin stronger, meaner, and colder, and it
made me wiser. Martin was out committing
crimes again; two months later, he would be
jailed again.

5   It is hard for me to imagine what I did
to myself, knowing that any day I could have
died senselessly. It is even harder for me to
accept the fact that my boyfriend would die
for a dirty, trashy street gang but not for

Topic   me. This last year I have been moving back to
sentence   the right track. I have gotten sober, started
college, and returned home. I have nightmares
about things I have seen and things I have
done. I struggle every day to stay sober, to
do the right thing. I am doing a lot of

Effects thinking. <u>I live each day in fear for
Martin's safety as well as my own.</u> I fear for
our future in a society that does not
understand us. I count down the days until
Martin can see the sunlight. <u>I pray every day
that this time will be the last time he goes
to jail.</u> <u>I pray Martin will trade his gun for
me, even get an education. I cry every night
and try to live every day.</u>

Exercise 3 Discussion and Critical Thinking

1. Why did McGraw become associated with Martin and finally become a gang member?

2. Were there deeper reasons for her dropping out of mainstream, middle-class society and joining a gang? Explain.

3. What were the effects on McGraw's life and the lives of those who were close to her?

4. What happened before the killing to set the stage for her change?

5. To what extent has McGraw changed?

6. Why doesn't she leave Martin? Discuss.

7. What is your reaction to the statement "I fear for our future in a society that does not understand us" (paragraph 5)?

Exercise 4 Suggestions for Reading-Based Writing

On separate paper, complete one of the following reading-based responses. Use references and quotations in reactions.

1. Write a summary of McGraw's essay.

2. Write a two-part response to McGraw's essay composed of labeled summary and reaction parts.

3. Write a reaction in which you examine each part of McGraw's experience and discuss the relationship of the parts. Concentrate on the stages of her changes for bad and good. As you emphasize stages, resist any temptation to write only a summary. Another approach would be to imagine that McGraw has written this essay to you, and now you are writing a paragraph of advice to her. Direct your advice to her through what she has written, using references and quotations.

Writer's Guidelines at a Glance: From Reading to Writing

1. Underlining helps you to read with discrimination.

   - Underline the main ideas in paragraphs.
   - Underline the support for those ideas.
   - Underline answers to questions that you bring to the reading assignment.
   - Underline only the key words.

2. Annotating enables you to actively engage the reading material.

   - Number parts if appropriate.
   - Make comments according to your interests and needs.

3. Summarizing helps you concentrate on main ideas. A summary

   - cites the author and title of the text.
   - is usually shorter than the original by about two-thirds, although the exact reduction will vary depending on the content of the original.

- concentrates on the main ideas and includes details only infrequently.
- changes the original wording without changing the idea.
- does not evaluate the content or give an opinion in any way (even if the original contains an error in logic or fact).
- does not add ideas (even if the writer of the summary has an abundance of related information).
- does not include any personal comments by the writer of the summary (therefore, no use of *I*, referring to self).
- seldom contains quotations (although, if it does, only with quotation marks).
- includes some author tags ("says York," "according to York," or "the author explains") to remind the reader(s) that it is a summary of the material of another writer.

4. Two other types of reading-based writing are

- the reaction, which shows how the reading relates to you, your experiences, and your attitudes, and, also, is often a critique of the worth and logic of the piece.
- the two-part response, which includes a summary and a reaction that are separate.

5. Most ideas in reading-based papers are developed in one or more of these three ways:

- explanation
- direct references
- quotations

6. Documenting is giving credit to borrowed ideas and words.

7. Reading-based writing requires you to read a source and to use it as a model of form and treatment of an idea.

8. Write and revise.

- Write and then revise your paragraph or essay as many times as necessary for **c**oherence, **l**anguage (usage, tone, and diction), **u**nity, **e**mphasis, **s**upport, and **s**entences (**CLUESS**). Read your work aloud to hear and correct any grammatical errors or awkward-sounding sentences.
- Edit any problems in fundamentals, such as **c**apitalization, **o**missions, **p**unctuation, and **s**pelling (**COPS**).

4

Paragraphs
and Essays

∿ Writing the Short Essay

The definition of a paragraph gives us a framework for defining the essay: A paragraph is a group of sentences, each with the function of supporting a single, main idea, which is contained in the topic sentence.

The key parts of a paragraph are the topic sentence (subject and focus), support (evidence and reasoning), and, often, the concluding sentence at the end. Now let's use that framework for an essay: An **essay** is a group of paragraphs, each with the function of stating or supporting a controlling idea called the thesis.

Following are the key parts of the essay:

Introduction: carries the thesis, which states the controlling idea—much like the topic sentence for a paragraph but on a larger scale—by giving the subject and focus

Development: evidence and reasoning—the support

Conclusion: an appropriate ending—often a restatement of or a reflection on the thesis

Thus, considered structurally, the paragraph is often an essay in miniature. That does not mean that all paragraphs can expand into essays or that all essays can shrink into paragraphs. For college writing, however, a good understanding of the parallel between well-organized paragraphs and well-organized essays is useful. As you learn the properties of effective paragraphs—those with a strong topic sentence and strong support—you also learn how to organize an essay, if you just magnify the procedure.

The diagram on page 55 illustrates the parallel parts of outlines, paragraphs, and essays:

Of course, the parallel components are not exactly the same in a paragraph and an essay. The paragraph is shorter and requires

54

much less development, and some paragraph topics simply couldn't be developed much more extensively to their advantage. But let's consider the ones that can. What happens? How do we proceed?

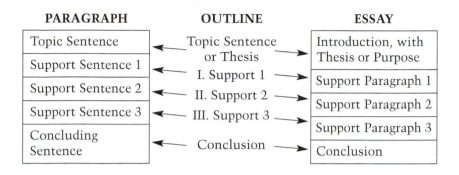

Introductory Paragraph

The topic-sentence idea is expanded to the introductory paragraph through elaboration: explanation, historical background, anecdote, quotation, or stress on the significance of an idea. Usually the introduction is three to six sentences long. If you say too much, your paper will be top-heavy. If you don't say enough, your readers will be confused. But a solid opening paragraph should

- introduce the subject through the thesis or controlling idea.
- gain reader interest.
- move the reader into the middle paragraphs. You should avoid any statement of apology about your topic or your writing and avoid beginning with a statement like "I am writing an essay about. . . ."

Middle Paragraphs

The middle paragraphs are similar to the paragraphs you have been writing. Each has its own unity based on the topic sentence, moves logically and coherently, and has adequate and appropriate development. The topic sentence is usually at the beginning of the paragraph in a college essay, regardless of the form. Although some essays are an expansion of a particular form of discourse and, therefore, use basically the same pattern for each paragraph, many essays combine the forms. For example, you might have one middle paragraph that

gives examples, one that defines, and one that classifies. You may
also have combinations within paragraphs. Nevertheless, the paragraphs are always related to the central idea and are presented in a
logical arrangement. The coherence of the paragraphs can often be
improved by the use of the same principles that you have applied
within each paragraph: using sequence words such as *first, second,*
and *third*; using transitional words such as *therefore, moreover,* and
for example; and arranging material in chronological order, spatial
order, or order of relative importance.

Concluding Paragraph

Like the introductory paragraph, the concluding paragraph is a
special unit with a specific function. In the concluding paragraph,
usually three to six sentences long, you end on a note of finality.
The way you end depends on what you want to do. If you can't decide on how to end, try going back to your introduction and see
what you said there. If you posed a question, the answer should be
in the conclusion. If you laid out the framework for an exploration
of the topic, then perhaps you will want to bring your discussion
together with a summary statement. Or maybe a quotation, an
anecdote, or a restatement of the thesis in slightly different words
would be effective. Do not end with a complaint, an apology, or
the introduction of a new topic or new support. And do not begin
your conclusion with the words such as "last but not least" or "in
conclusion." Try for a fresh approach.

Examining a Paragraph and an Essay

Student Writing

Here is the paragraph, followed by the essay on page 58.

Superman and Batman (paragraph)

Judy Urbina

Topic sentence (subject, focus)	Both Superman and Batman are heroes, but only one is truly a superhero, and taking into account their upbringing, motives, and criminal targets, that is Batman. Upbringing

I. Upbringing **A. Superman**	was not gentle for either. Superman came from Krypton, a planet that was about to self-destruct. His parents sent him as a baby on a spaceship to Earth. There he would be adopted by an ordinary farm family. His adoptive parents named him Clark Kent and reared him well. In the same generation, far away in
B. Batman	Gotham, Bruce Wayne, the future Batman, was born to a contented, wealthy family. Tragically, his parents were killed in his presence during a mugging. He inherited the family wealth and was raised by his kindly butler. Those very different backgrounds provided Superman and Batman with powerful
II. Motives	but different motives for fighting crime.
A. Superman	Superman was programmed in his space capsule to know about the forces of good and evil on Earth and to fight the bad people. Unlike
B. Batman	Superman, Batman learned from experience. Both have gone on to fight many bad people,
III. Enemies	but each one has a special enemy. For
A. Superman	Superman, it is Lex Luthor, who has studied Superman and knows all about him, even his outstanding weakness—the mineral Kryptonite.
B. Batman	For Batman, it is the Joker, who, as a wicked teenager, was the mugger-murderer of Batman's parents. Many spectacular battles have ensued for both crime fighters, and one has reached the top in his profession. Superman offers overwhelming physical strength against crime, but Batman displays cunning and base passion. As he strikes fear in the hearts of the
Concluding **statement**	wicked, he's not just winning; he is getting even. Most people would cheer Superman on. However, they would identify more with Batman, and he is the superhero.

Superman and Batman (essay)

Judy Urbina

1   During the Depression in the 1930s,
Superman and Batman were created as the
first big comic-book heroes. More than two
thousand similar but lesser characters
were to follow. Both Superman and Batman
have been enormously successful, but one
seems to have more personality and is
probably closer to most of us emotionally.
Which hero wins out in this struggle for

Thesis our hearts and minds? Taking into account
(subject, their upbringing, motives, and criminal
focus) targets, one can argue that it is Batman
who is more credible.

2   Neither came originally from a home
I. Upbringing environment we are likely to identify with
A. Superman completely. Superman was conceived on the
planet Krypton by a highly intelligent
couple. His life was threatened because
Krypton was going to destruct. Superman's
parents bundled him up in a kiddie
spacecraft and launched him on a long
journey to Earth to save his life. He was
raised on a farm by Jonathan and Martha
Kent, who adopted him and grew to love him
B. Batman as their own. Batman, however, had an
upbringing which we can more easily
imagine as a complete pattern. Really
Bruce Wayne in disguise, Batman was left
an orphan by his parents, who were killed
in a mugging right in front of him.
Fortunately for Bruce Wayne, his parents
were rich, and he inherited millions when
they died. He was raised by his butler,

unlike Superman, who was nurtured by a conventional adoptive mom and dad. Obviously the upbringing of these two heroes had a lot to do with the kind of heroes they grew up to be.

II. Motives   3   Both comic-book heroes had different motives for confronting killers and

A. Superman   spoilers. Superman instinctively knew he was sent to Earth to fight crime. When his birth parents shipped him off to Earth as an infant, they programmed the spacecraft to educate him on the ways of the Earthlings. Superman's adoptive parents reinforced those lessons by teaching him that he had to hide his powers and use them for the well-being of the human race.

B. Batman   To the contrary, Batman soon became a revenge-driven vigilante after his parents were killed in the mugging, so he decided to devote his life to fighting crime, with his butler as a domestic accomplice. To Batman no criminal is a good criminal. Although all of us citizens know we should not take the law into our own hands, nevertheless, we celebrate Superman and Batman as heroes, all the time identifying more with the guy in the fancy bat car.

III. Enemies   4   Like all superheroes, each of these

A. Superman   two has an archenemy. Superman's archenemy is Lex Luthor, who has a brilliant criminal mind. Lex Luthor is always trying to destroy Superman. He knows everything about Superman, right down to his

B. Batman   weakness—the mineral Kryptonite. Batman's main enemy is the Joker. As a teen, the Joker killed Batman's parents. Then Batman

"accidentally" dropped the Joker into acid
and permanently disfigured his face, so
they are constantly getting into battles.
More people are able to relate to Batman
because most of us at least think about
vengeance if someone has done us wrong.
Superman just wants to fight for "truth,
justice, and the American way," all
worthwhile values, but they're abstract.

5   Superman does not offer love or self-
knowledge as keys to a perfect world. He
offers only physical strength. Displaying
more cunning and base passion, Batman
preys on fears and insecurities of
criminals as keys to a perfect world. He
wants to keep the bad men and women
intimidated and on the run. His presence
in Gotham strikes fear in the hearts of
the wicked. Neither crime fighter is much
concerned about rehabilitation. Mainly
they knock heads. But Batman seems to
enjoy his work more than Superman because
Batman's getting even. The fact that we
are in touch with that source of
satisfaction says as much about us as it
does about Batman.

Exercise 1 Expanding a Paragraph into an Essay

*The following paragraph could easily be expanded into an essay
because the topic sentence and its related statements can be developed into an introduction; each of the main divisions (five) can
be expanded into a separate paragraph; and the restated topic
sentence can, with elaboration, become the concluding paragraph.
Divide the following paragraph with the symbol ¶ and annotate it
in the left-hand margin with the words* Introduction, Support *(and*

numbers for the middle five paragraphs), and Conclusion *to show the parts that would be developed further. The topic sentence has been marked for you.*

What Is a Gang?

Will Cusak

Topic sentence with related statements

The word *gang* is often used loosely to mean "a group of people who go around together," but that does not satisfy the concerns of law-enforcement people and sociologists. For these professionals, the definition of *gang* has five parts. These five parts combine to form a unit. First, a gang has to have a name. Some well-known gang names are Bloods, Crips, Hell's Angels, and Mexican Mafia. The second part of the definition is clothing or other identifying items, such as tattoos. The clothing may be of specific brands or colors, such as blue for Crips and red for Bloods. Members of the Aryan Brotherhood often have blue thunderbolt tattoos. A third component is rituals. They may involve such things as the use of handshakes, other body language or signing, and graffiti. A fourth is binding membership. A gang member is part of an organization, a kind of family, with obligations and codes of behavior to follow. Finally, a gang will be involved in some criminal behavior, something such as prostitution, drugs, thievery, or burglary. There are many different kinds of gangs—ethnic, regional, behavioral—but they all have these five characteristics.

〜 Topics for Short Essays

Many paragraph topics in this book can become topics for short essays. Look through the lists of Reading-Based Writing Topics, General Topics, Cross-Curricular Topics, and Career-Related Topics at the end of Chapters 5 through 13 to find ideas that can be expanded. Here are some ways to accomplish the expansion.

> **Narration:** Expand each part of the narrative form (situation, conflict, struggle, outcome, and meaning) into one or more paragraphs. Give the most emphasis to the struggle.
>
> **Description:** Expand each unit of descriptive detail into a paragraph. All paragraphs should support the dominant impression.
>
> **Exemplification:** Expand one example into an extended example or expand a group of examples into separate paragraphs. Each paragraph should support the main point.
>
> **Analysis by division:** Expand the discussion by treating each part of the unit in a separate paragraph.
>
> **Process analysis:** Expand the preparation and each step in the process into a separate paragraph.
>
> **Cause and effect:** Expand each cause or effect into a separate paragraph.
>
> **Comparison and contrast:** In the point-by-point pattern, expand each point into a separate paragraph. In the subject-by-subject pattern, first expand each subject into a separate paragraph. If you have sufficient material on each point, you can also expand each point into a separate paragraph.
>
> **Definition:** Expand each aspect of the definition (characteristics, examples, and comparative points) into a separate paragraph.
>
> **Argument:** Expand the refutation and each main division of support into a separate paragraph.

Of course, the statement that a paragraph is seldom made up of a single pattern also applies to the essay. Most essays have a combination of patterns, although one pattern may prevail and provide the main structure. Therefore, any topic selected from the end-of-chapter suggestions should be developed with an open mind about possibilities of using more than one pattern of development.

Writer's Guidelines at a Glance: Paragraphs and Essays

You do not usually set out to write an essay by
first writing a paragraph. But the organization
for the paragraph and the essay is often the same, and the writing
process is also the same. You still proceed from prewriting to topic,
to outline, to draft, to revising, to editing, to final paper. The difference is often only a matter of development and indentation.

1. The well-designed paragraph and the well-designed essay often
   have the same form.
   a. The **introduction** carries the thesis, which states the control-
      ling idea—much like the topic sentence for a paragraph but on
      a larger scale.
   b. The development, or middle part, supplies evidence and
      reasoning—the **support**.
   c. The **conclusion** provides an appropriate ending—often a
      restatement of, or reflection on, the thesis.
2. The following diagram shows the important relationships
   among the paragraph, outline, and essay.

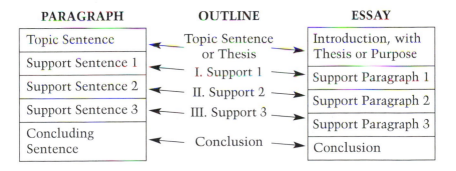

5

Narration: Moving
Through Time

⌒ Writing Paragraphs of Narration

In our everyday lives, we tell stories and invite other people to do so by asking questions such as "What happened at work today?" and "What did you do last weekend?" We are disappointed when the answer is "Nothing much." We may be equally disappointed when a person doesn't give us enough details or gives us too many and spoils the effect. After all, we are interested in people's stories and in the people who tell them. We like narratives.

What is a narrative? A **narrative** is an account of an incident or a series of incidents that make up a complete and significant action. A narrative can be as short as a joke, as long as a novel, or anything in between, including a single paragraph. Each narrative has five properties: situation, conflict, struggle, outcome, and meaning.

Situation

Situation is the background for the action. The situation may be described only briefly, or it may even be implied. ("To celebrate my seventeenth birthday, I went to the Department of Motor Vehicles to take my practical test for my driver's license.")

Conflict

Conflict is friction, such as a problem in the surroundings, with another person(s), or within the individual. The conflict, which is at the heart of each story, produces struggle. ("It was raining and my appointment was the last one of the day. The examiner was a serious, weary-looking man who reminded me of a bad boss I once had, and I was nervous.")

64

Struggle

Struggle, which need not be physical, is the manner of dealing with the conflict. The struggle adds action or engagement and generates the plot. ("After grinding on the ignition because the engine was already on, I had trouble finding the windshield wiper control. Next I forgot to signal until after I had pulled away from the curb. As we crept slowly down the rain-glazed street, the examiner told me to take the emergency brake off. All the while I listened to his pen scratching on his clipboard. 'Pull over and park,' he said solemnly.")

Outcome

Outcome is the result of the struggle. ("After I parked the car, the examiner told me to relax, and then he talked to me about school. When we continued, somehow I didn't make any errors, and I got my license.")

Meaning

Meaning is the significance of the story, which may be deeply philosophical or simple, stated or implied. ("Calmness promotes calmness.") Most narratives written as college assignments have an expository purpose (that is, they explain a specified idea). Often the narrative will be merely an extended example. Therefore, the meaning of the narrative is exceedingly important and should be clear, whether it is stated or implied.

These five properties are present in some way in all the many forms of the narrative. They are often enhanced by the use of various devices such as the following:

- **Description** (the use of specific details to advance action, with images to make readers see, smell, taste, hear, and feel)

  the *rain-glazed street*

  listened to his *pen scratching*

- **Dialogue** (the exact words of the speakers, enclosed in quotation marks)

  "*Pull over and park,*" he said solemnly.

Transitional Words

Consider using the following transitional words to improve coherence by connecting ideas with ideas, sentences with sentences, and paragraphs with paragraphs:

- **FOR NARRATION   Time:** *after, before, later, earlier, initially, soon, recently, next, today, tomorrow, yesterday, now, then, until, currently, when, finally, not long after, immediately, (at) first, (at) last, third, previously, in the meantime, meanwhile*

- **FOR DESCRIPTION AS PART OF NARRATION   Place:** *above, over, under, below, nearby, near, across, beyond, among, to the right, to the left, in the background, in the foreground, further, beside, opposite, within sight, out of sight*

Practicing Patterns of Narration

Exercise 1 Completing Patterns

Fill in the blanks to complete each narrative pattern.

1. Lost and Found Surprise

   (situation)   I. Person taking store money deposit bag to bank

   (conflict)   II. Person loses bag

   (struggle)   III. _____

   (outcome)   IV. _____

   (meaning)   V. _____

2. Good Samaritan Appears

   (situation)   I. Driver with flat tire, dead of night

   (conflict)   II. No spare tire

   (struggle)   III. _____

   (outcome)   IV. _____

   (meaning)   V. _____

～ Examining Paragraphs of Narration

Student Writing

King of Klutziness

Joel Bailey

We begin with a humorous paragraph by student writer Joel Bailey, who gives an account of his clumsiness as a worker in a fast-food establishment.

Topic sentence	It was my first task of what would be a memorable day at work in Carl's Jr., a fast-
Place	food place by <u>Universal Studio</u> near Hollywood. I was assigned to the front counter because another worker was late.
Situation	There I was at <u>noon</u>, the busiest time of the
Time	day, with no training, scared, and nervous. In the beginning, things went well. Orders were routine, and I filled them and made
Transition	change. <u>As time passed</u>, the lines got short, and I was still doing great because, after all, the job didn't require the mentality of a rocket scientist. Several counter people left their registers to help out in back.
Transition	<u>Then</u> a lot of people came in at one time.
Conflict	Only two of us were taking orders. I was nervous. I served three persons, hardly looking up as I punched the keys, called out
Transition	orders, and made change. <u>After</u> barely
Image: sound	glancing at the next person, <u>I heard his voice</u> ordering, a familiar voice. It was Alex Benson, a reporter for a TV channel I frequently watched. I repeated his order to him so that it would be perfect, and I took
Transition	his money. <u>After</u> I gave him his change, he
Struggle	stared at the receipt and said with more than a touch of irritation, "<u>You made a mistake.</u>

	You charged me for two chicken burgers." I
	apologized and gave him a refund. "What about
Dialogue	the tax," he growled. "You didn't refund the
	tax." I was really getting nervous. He always
	laughed and smiled on TV. I gave him the tax
	money. I grabbed someone else's chicken order
	just so I could give him quick service, but
	when I handed him the tray, my hand slipped
	and I spilled his Coke on his trousers.
	Quickly I grabbed a napkin and ran around the
Outcome	counter and wiped at the Coke stain.
Image: sight	Unfortunately the napkin I grabbed had catsup
Transition	on it. Now I had added a condiment to the
	Coke stain. By that time I might as well have
	salted and peppered him. Beyond anger, and
Meaning	looking at me wildly, he fled with his tray
	to a distant booth and sat with his back to
	the wall. I decided not to ask for an
	autograph.

Yearning for Love

Chantra Shastri

Having lived in the United States for five years, Chantra Shastri asks for freedom—freedom to make a choice in marriage, a choice based on love.

	I need not go beyond myself to find
	examples of love, at least the yearning for
	love. My home is now America, but I have not
	left India far behind. There, in ways still
Situation	cherished by my traditional family, freedom
	is based on gender, and I am a female. My
	parents expect women to cook, clean, and
Conflict	nurture. My parents expect me to marry the
	man of their choice, although my brother will

	have the freedom to choose his own mate. If I
	disobey, I will no longer be recognized by my
	parents. It is easy to give in to such a
Struggle	custom; it is difficult to disobey. My
	parents have always believed as they do. I
	cannot change them, nor do I want to, but I
	wish they would accept my difference in this
	different country. I think my mother
Transition	understands. <u>Last week</u>, I saw her crying
(focus within a	while she ironed our clothes. When I asked
narration)	her why she was crying, she wiped the warm
	tears off her thin, soft cheeks and pretended
	not to hear me as she sang. Her singing made
	me sad because I knew why she had cried, and
	she knew I knew. I seized the opportunity to
Dialogue	say, "I don't want an arranged marriage," but
	she sang on even louder, singing a song of a
	distant home. In times such as these, like my
Outcome	father, she too covers her ears with the
	thick dried mud of tradition. She doesn't
Meaning	want to hear me. It is easier that way.

Exercise 2 Discussion and Critical Thinking

1. Why did Shastri's mother cry?

2. What chance does Shastri have to make her own choice?

3. What would you advise her to do?

4. How does the specific example of Shastri's mother crying imply more than it actually says?

Professional Writing

Voice Like Twigs Underfoot

Maxine Hong Kingston

> *Now a celebrated writer, Maxine Hong Kingston was once so deficient in English speech that she flunked kindergarten. In this passage taken from her book* The Woman Warrior: Memoirs of a Childhood Among Ghosts *(1976), she tells about one of her early experiences as a frightened girl caught between two cultures.*

Not all of the children who were silent at American school found voice at Chinese school.† One new teacher said each of us had to get up and recite in front of the class, who was to listen. My sister and I had memorized the lesson perfectly. We said it to

Image: Sound each other at home, one chanting, one listening. The teacher called on my sister to recite first. It was the first time a teacher had called on the second-born to go first. My sister was scared. She glanced at me and looked away; I looked down at my desk. I hoped that she could do it because if she could, then I would have to. She opened her mouth and a voice came out

Image: Sound that wasn't a whisper, but it wasn't a proper voice either. I hoped that she would not cry, fear breaking up her voice like twigs underfoot. She sounded as if she

Image: Sound were trying to sing through weeping and strangling. She did not pause or stop to end the embarrassment. She kept going until she said the last word, and then she sat down. When it was my turn, the same voice

Image: Sound
came out, a crippled animal running on broken legs. You could hear splinters in my voice, bones rubbing jagged against one another. I was loud, though. I was glad I didn't whisper.

Exercise 3 Discussion and Critical Thinking

In your own words, identify the following parts of Kingston's narrative.

Situation: _____

Conflict: _____

Struggle: _____

Outcome: _____

Meaning: _____

∼ Topics for Paragraphs of Narration

Most of these topics can also be used for short essays.

Reading-Based Writing Topics

See Chapter 3 for instruction and examples for writing summaries, reactions, and two-part responses (separate paragraphs of summary and reaction). Use quotations and references. Credit source(s).

"Yearning for Love"

1. Assume that you are a psychologist or the personal-advice columnist for a large newspaper and Chantra Shastri has written her paragraph to you. Realizing that she has a life ahead of her and her family is asking her to choose between independence and family, what would you suggest that she do? Another possible aspect of the issue: Take into account that Shastri's parents might say to you that most American marriages end in divorce and that they, the parents, could make a better decision for a sound marriage, one that is less immature, less emotional, and less hormonal—one that is based on what they know about both their daughter and the young man they had already selected? Refer directly to the paragraph and use quotations.

"Voice Like Twigs Underfoot"

2. Write a narrative paragraph about something you had to struggle to do, like make a presentation or talk to someone you admired, held in high esteem, or were afraid of. Make this paragraph reading based by using references and quotations to comment on how your fear was similar to that of Maxine Hong Kingston.

General Topics

3. Write a narrative paragraph about the first time you did something, such as the first time you dated, kissed romantically, spoke formally in public, entered a new school, worked for pay, drove an automobile, rode a bicycle or motorcycle, danced, received a traffic citation, met a celebrity, tried out for a sports team or a club or other "social" group, confessed you did something wrong, applied for a job, or met your date's parents. For a helpful model on a similar topic, review "Voice Like Twigs Underfoot" on page 70.
4. Write a narrative paragraph about a personal experience that you might characterize as the most amusing, sad, terrifying, satisfying, stupid, rewarding, self-centered, generous, stingy, loving, thoughtful, cruel, regrettable, educational, corrupting, sinful, virtuous, or disgusting thing you have done or witnessed. Keep in mind that you are writing about a single event or a portion of that event. For a helpful model on a similar topic, review "Voice Like Twigs Underfoot" on page 70.

Cross-Curricular Topics

5. Write a case study of an individual's behavior in a class requiring observation, such as teacher training, physical education, sociology, psychology, or business management.
6. Write a report on how you completed an experiment in a class (biology, ecology, psychology).
7. Describe a pivotal moment or revealing incident in the life of a historical figure, a composer, an artist, or an author.

Career-Related Topics

8. Write a narrative paragraph about learning how to do something specific on the job. In what way(s) did you or someone else perform badly, perhaps ridiculously? Many of these events

occur on the first day of employment. For a helpful model on a similar topic, review "King of Klutziness" on page 67.

9. Write a narrative paragraph about a work-related encounter between a manager and a worker, and briefly explain the significance of the event.
10. Write a narrative paragraph about an encounter between a customer and a salesperson. Explain what went right and what went wrong.
11. Write a narrative paragraph about how a person solved a work-related problem.
12. Write a narrative paragraph about a salesperson's dealing with a customer's complaint. Critique the procedure.

Writer's Guidelines at a Glance: Narration

1. Use this checklist to be sure you have a complete narrative.

   ☐ Situation (at beginning)
   ☐ Conflict
   ☐ Struggle
   ☐ Outcome
   ☐ Meaning

2. Use these devices as appropriate:

   - Images (sight, sound, smell, taste, touch) and other details to advance action
   - Dialogue
   - Transitional words (such as *after, finally, following, later, next, soon, when*) to enhance chronological order

3. Use CLUESS for revision and COPS for editing. See pages 21–24 for guidance.

6

Description:
Moving Through
Space and Time

∼ Writing Paragraphs of Description

Description is the use of words to represent the appearance or nature of something. Often called a **word picture**, description attempts to present its subject for the mind's eye. In doing so, it does not merely become an indifferent camera; instead, it selects details that will depict something well. Just what details the descriptive writer selects will depend on several factors, especially the type of description and the dominant impression in the passage.

Types of Description

On the basis of treatment of subject material, description is customarily divided into two types: objective and subjective.

Effective **objective description** presents the subject clearly and directly as it exists outside the realm of feelings. If you are explaining the function of the heart, the characteristics of a computer chip, or the renovation of a manufacturing facility, your description would probably feature specific, impersonal details. Most technical and scientific writing is objective in that sense. It is likely to be practical and utilitarian, making little use of speculation and poetic technique while focusing on details of sight.

Effective **subjective description** is also concerned with clarity and it may be direct, but it conveys a feeling about the subject and sets a mood while making a point. Because most expression involves personal views, even when it explains by analysis, subjective description (often called **emotional description**) has a broader range of uses than objective description.

74

Descriptive passages can be a combination of objective and subjective description; only the larger context of the passage will reveal the main intent. The following description of a baseball begins with objective treatment and then moves to subjective.

On the Ball

Roger Angell

[A baseball] weighs just over five ounces and measures between 2.86 and 2.94 inches in diameter. It is made of a composition-cork nucleus encased in two thin layers of rubber, one black and one red, surrounded by 121 yards of tightly wrapped blue-gray wool yarn, 45 yards of white wool yarn, 53 more yards of blue-gray wool yarn, 150 yards of fine cotton yarn, a coat of rubber cement, and a cowhide (formerly horsehide) exterior, which is held together with 216 slightly raised cotton stitches. Printed certifications, endorsements, and outdoor advertising spherically attest to its authenticity. . . . Pick it up and it instantly suggests its purpose; it is meant to be thrown a considerable distance—thrown hard and with precision. Its feel and heft are the beginning of the sport's critical dimensions; if it were a fraction of an inch larger or smaller, a few centigrams heavier or lighter, the game of baseball would be utterly different. Hold a baseball in your hand. As it happens, this one is not brand-new. Here, just to one side of the curved surgical welt of stitches, there is a pale-green grass smudge, darkening on one edge almost to black—the mark of an old infield play, a tough grounder now lost in memory. Feel the ball, turn it over in your hand; hold it across the seam or the other way, with the seam just to the side of your middle finger. Speculation stirs. You want to get outdoors and throw this spare and sensual object to somebody or, at the very least, watch somebody else throw it. The game has begun.

Imagery

To convey your main concern effectively to readers, you will have to give some sensory impressions. These sensory impressions, collectively called **imagery**, refer to that which can be experienced by the senses—what we can see, smell, taste, hear, and touch.

Subjective description is more likely to use images and words rich in associations than is objective description. But just as a fine line cannot always be drawn between the objective and the subjective, a fine line cannot always be drawn between word choice in one and in the other. However, we can say with certainty that whatever the type of description, careful word choice will always be important.

General and Specific Words

To move from the general to the specific is to move from the whole class or body to the individual(s); for example:

General	Specific	More Specific
food	pastry	Twinkie
mess	grease	oil slicks on table
drink	soda	mug of root beer
odor	smell from grill	smell of frying onions

Abstract and Concrete Words

Words are classified as abstract or concrete depending on what they refer to. **Abstract words** refer to qualities or ideas: *good, ordinary, ultimate, truth, beauty, maturity, love.* **Concrete words** refer to substances or things; they have reality: *onions, grease, buns, tables, food.* The specific concrete words, sometimes called **concrete particulars**, often support generalizations effectively and convince the reader of the accuracy of the account.

Dominant Impression

Never try to give all of the details in description; instead, be selective, picking only those that you need to make a dominant impression, always taking into account the knowledge and attitudes of your readers. Remember, description is not photographic. If you wish to describe a person, select only those traits that will present the person according to your concerns. If you wish to describe a landscape, do not give all the details that you might find in a photo; just pick the details that support what you want to say. That extremely important dominant impression is directly linked to your purpose and is created by choosing and arranging images and other revealing details.

Order: Time and Space

All of these details must have some order. Time and space are the main controlling factors in most description.

If you were describing something that was not changing—a room, for example—you would be concerned with space and give directions to the reader such as *next to, below, under, above, be-hind, in front of, beyond, in the foreground, in the background, to the left,* or *to the right.*

If you were describing something that was changing, such as a butterfly going through metamorphosis, you would be concerned mainly with time and use transitional words such as *first, second, then, soon, finally, while, after, next, later, now,* or *before.*

If you were walking through an area—so that the setting was changing—you would use both time and space for order.

Transitional Words

Consider using the following transitional words to improve coherence by connecting ideas with ideas, sentences with sentences, and paragraphs with paragraphs:

- **FOR DESCRIPTION   Place:** *above, over, under, below, nearby, near, across, beyond, among, to the right, to the left, in the background, in the foreground, further, beside, opposite, within sight, out of sight*

- **FOR NARRATION AS A FRAMEWORK FOR DESCRIPTION Time:** *after, before, later, earlier, initially, soon, recently, next, today, tomorrow, yesterday, now, then, until, currently, when, finally, not long after, immediately, (at) first, (at) last, third, previously, in the meantime, meanwhile*

Procedure at a Glance

What is your subject? (school campus during summer vacation)
What is the dominant impression? (deserted)
What details support the dominant impression?

1. Smell of flowers and cut grass rather than food and smoke and perfume
2. Dust accumulated on white porcelain drinking fountain
3. Sound of the wind, wildlife, and silence rather than people
4. Crunch of dead leaves underfoot
5. Echo of footsteps

What is the situation? (You are walking across the campus in early August.)
What is the order of details? (time and place)

◠ Practicing Patterns of Description

Exercise 1 Completing Patterns

Fill in the blanks in the following outline to complete the description.

Shopping in a Supermarket Produce Area
(Dominant impression: Diversity of products)

   I. Food displays (sight—color, shape)

      A. _____

      B. _____

      C. _____

  II. Smells (from vegetables, fruits)

      A. _____

      B. _____

 III. Textures (smooth or rough to touch)

      A. _____

      B. _____

 IV. Taste (samples of sweet/sour, ripe/unripe)

      A. _____

      B. _____

◠ Examining Paragraphs of Description

Student Writing

My Burning Scarf

Julie Lee

Student Julie Lee writes about a scarf that was mistakenly burned in a family ceremony. Her attention to descriptive detail highlights this vivid recollection and conveys the poignancy of her experience. Be prepared to discuss this as narration.

Dominant impression	During my childhood, my <u>favorite</u> <u>possession</u> was the yellow scarf my dad gave me
Topic sentence	when I was five. <u>It would bring me pleasure and</u> <u>pain</u>. Hand-sewn with care in Japan, it attracted many curious and envious eyes. Needless to say, I was the proud owner of that scarf and loved the attention it brought me.
Objective descriptive details	The scarf was <u>about two feet square and made of</u> <u>pure virgin wool</u>. <u>It was decorated with a</u> <u>fringed green edge, and in one corner five</u>
Images: sight	<u>embroidered yellow-colored chicks played</u> <u>against the background needlework of lush green</u>
Images: touch	grass. The material was as <u>soft as cashmere</u> and had the <u>warmth of fur</u>. It kept my cheeks warm when I wrapped it loosely around my neck. But when I was six, I let my seriously ill sister wear my scarf to the doctor's office. She didn't give it back to me immediately, and because she was sick I didn't ask for it. Sadly, she died of leukemia after months of suffering. A few days after she died, from my
Images: sight	bedroom, I <u>saw my mother</u> in the backyard <u>burning personal items</u> that belonged to my dead sister. It is a Korean custom to do so. My mother was crying and so were other adults standing in a circle around the fire. Then I
Images: sight	saw my mother pick up my <u>wadded yellow scarf</u> and shake it out. I rushed outside, <u>shrieking</u>
Images: sound	for her to stop. Over the sounds of <u>sobbing</u> and the <u>popping</u> of the fire, I wanted to shout, "That's my scarf, my precious possession." But I didn't, and my mother, thinking I was crying only for my sister, flung it into the flames of
Images: sound	the fire that <u>sizzled and cracked</u>, and the green and yellow of my childhood turned to orange, then red, then gray.

The Drag

Mike Kavanagh

When student Mike Kavanagh looked at the assignment to write a descriptive paragraph about something he knew well, he had no trouble selecting a subject. As a drag racer for sport and prize money, he had built up his car, a 1968 Camaro, to thunder down the track at more than two hundred miles per hour, with all his senses raw to the wind.

The outline in the left margin shows how narration can provide a framework for descriptive details.

**Topic
sentence**

As I climb into the cockpit for my drag, I hear the roar of the crowd and the thundering blasts in the background. Engulfed

I. Preparation
**A. Take
position**
B. Strap in
**1. Straps
merge**
2. Buckle

in an iron cage, I strap myself down. First over the shoulders, then from the waist, and finally from between my legs the straps merge and then buckle at my belly button. This is to ensure my stability in the ironclad, two-hundred-and-thirty-miles-per-hour street rocket. My crew then signals me to fire up

II. Warm up
**A. Fire
motor**
**1. Feel
rumble**
**2. Hear
blower**
**3. Smell
nitro**
**B. Dry hop
tires**

the three thousand horsepower motor mounted at my back. With the push of a button, I feel the rumble of the motor, hear the scream of the blower, and smell the distinctive odor of nitro in the air. I then move up to the starting line to dry hop my rear tires for

**Descriptive
with narrative
frame**

better traction. I quickly thrust the accelerator pedal to the floor. I am shot forward about two hundred feet. Letting off the accelerator pedal and pulling the brake handle allows me to come to a slow stop. A low continuous thump from the motor echoes through my head as I reverse back to the starting line. As I creep forward, I stage

III. Drag
**A. Green
light**
B. Thrust

the beast and wait for the lights to change to green. This feels like an eternity. The lights flicker yellow, yellow, yellow, GREEN!

C. Braking
  1. Regular brakes
  2. Parachutes
D. Success
  1. Scoreboard
  2. Feeling

I stab the pedal to the floor. I am flung thirteen hundred and twenty feet faster than I can say my name. When I pull the brake and parachute handles simultaneously, I lunge back from the force of the billowing chutes. I climb out of the jungle gym and look up at the scoreboard, which reads 5.26 seconds at 230.57. There's nothing else like rocketing down the track at that speed!

Exercise 2 Discussion and Critical Thinking

1. Is this paragraph mainly descriptive, mainly narrative, or equally balanced? Discuss.

2. Although you probably have not drag raced competitively, you can get a good feeling of what it is like to do so by reading this paragraph. What details and what phrasing convince you that the author is writing from experience? Discuss.

3. What is the dominant impression and how is it supported?

4. List four words of transition used in the first five sentences.

Professional Writing

The Road to Cedar City

William Least Heat-Moon

William Trogdon, of English-Irish-Osage ancestry, writes under the pen name William Least Heat-Moon. Traveling around the country in an old van he named Ghost Dancing, he sought out interesting locales on secondary highways marked in blue on road maps. His descriptive narratives of these adventures were published in the best-selling book Blue Highways, *from which this paragraph is taken.*

At dusk I considered going to the Coral Sand Dunes for the night, but I'd had enough warmth and desert for a while, so I pushed north toward Cedar Breaks in the severe and beautiful Markagunt Plateau. The cool would refresh me. Sporadic splats of rain, not enough to pay attention to, hit the windshield. I turned onto Utah 14, the cross-mountain road to Cedar City. In the dim light of a mountainous sky, I could just make out a large sign.

ELEVATION 10,000 FEET
ROAD MAY BE IMPASSABLE
DURING WINTER MONTHS.

So? It was nearly May. The rain popped, then stopped, popped and stopped. The incline became steeper and light rain fell steadily, rolling red desert dust off the roof; I hadn't hit showers since east Texas. It was good. The pleasant cool turned to cold, and I switched on the heater. The headlights glared off snow-banks edging closer to the highway as it climbed, and the rain became sleet. That's when I began thinking I might have made a little miscalculation. I looked for a place to turn around, but there was only narrow, twisted road. The sleet got heavier, and the headlights were cutting only thirty feet into it. Maybe I could drive above and out of the storm. At eight thousand feet, the wind came up—a rough, nasty wind that bullied me about the slick road. Lear,* daring the storm to "strike flat the thick rotundity of the world," cries, "Blow, winds!...Rage! Blow!" And that's just what they did.

*The main character in William Shakespeare's play *King Lear*.

Exercise 3 Discussion and Critical Thinking

1. What is the dominant impression of the descriptive paragraph by William Least Heat-Moon?

2. What support does he use for the dominant impression?

3. Give an example of each of these kinds of images:

   Sight:

   Sound:

   Touch:

4. Is the description organized by time or space or both? Explain.

⌇ Topics for Paragraphs of Description

Most of these topics can also be used for short essays.

Reading-Based Writing Topics

See Chapter 3 for instruction and examples for writing summaries, reactions, and two-part responses (separate paragraphs of summary and reaction). Use quotations and references. Credit source(s).

"My Burning Scarf"

1. Write a reaction to this descriptive paragraph in which you explain how the meaning incorporates personal needs, family, and culture (perhaps using those headings for your outline). Explain how Lee's use of a narrative framework makes the passage more compelling. As an option, you could use the narrative framework (situation, conflict, struggle, outcome, and meaning) as main points in your outline for discussing this paragraph. Use references and quotations.

"The Drag"

2. Write a reaction to this paragraph in which you explain how the author made this passage vivid and compelling by using techniques of writing description and narration. Consider using the basic pattern of narration (situation, conflict, struggle, outcome, meaning) to show progression along with the description. Include comments on the dominant impression and images (sight, sound, smell, touch). Use references and quotations.

General Topics

Objective Description

3. Describe a ball (other than a baseball)—basketball, golf ball, tennis ball, soccer ball—or other piece of sports equipment that can be depicted objectively but often inspires a subjective reaction. It might be helpful to include a photo or a drawing of your subject. For a useful model on a similar subject, review "On the Ball" on page 75.

Subjective Description

4. Write a highly descriptive paragraph about a possession you received or purchased, treasured, and—somehow—lost, perhaps through theft, your carelessness, wear and tear, or someone else's neglect or spiteful act. Describe it well, but locate the possession within the framework of a little story. For a useful model on a similar subject, review "My Burning Scarf" on page 78.

5. Describe an exciting moment you experienced; it need not be a sporting event, but it can be. It could be an accident, a rescue, an unexpected pleasure, or any personal triumph. Pick an event you can describe colorfully. For a useful model paragraph on a similar subject, review "The Drag" on page 80.

6. Describe a dramatic part of a difficult adventure you have experienced. It might be a difficult trip you took (as a driver or as a passenger, perhaps with an impaired driver) under bad conditions, such as fog, snow, rain, windstorm, hail, heat, or traffic congestion. Or it could be a scary walk or run you took in the darkness, in a remote area, or in any area that made you fearful. Consider quoting from any warning someone gave you prior to the adventure or any sign you encountered along the way. For a useful model paragraph on a similar subject, review "The Road to Cedar City" on page 82.

7. Personalize a trip to a supermarket, a stadium, an airport, an unusual house, a mall, a beach, a court, a place of worship, a club, a business, a library, or a police station. Describe a simple conflict in one of those places, while emphasizing descriptive details.

8. Pick a high point in any event, and describe a few seconds of it. Think about how a scene can be captured by a video camera, and then give focus by applying the dominant-impression principle, using the images of sight, sound, taste, touch, and smell that are relevant. The event might be a ball game, a graduation ceremony, a wedding ceremony, a funeral, a dance, a concert, a family gathering, a class meeting, a rally, a riot, a robbery, a fight, a proposal, or a meal. Focus on a body of subject material that you can cover effectively in the paragraph you write.

Cross-Curricular Topic

9. Select one of the following assignments, then use description to write the report.

   a. Agriculture: Field-trip report
   b. Art History: Report on a museum or a particular work of art
   c. Education: School-visit report
   d. Ecology: Field-trip report
   e. Geology: Field-trip report
   f. Sociology: Report on a field trip to an urban zone, a prison, or another institution

Career-Related Topics

10. Describe a well-furnished, well-functioning office or other work area. Be specific.

11. Describe a product, with special attention to the dominant trait that gives the product its reputation.

12. Describe a person properly groomed and attired for a particular job or interview. Be specific in giving details pertaining to the person and in naming the place or situation. If you like, objectively describe yourself (to the best of your ability) as that specific person.

Writer's Guidelines at a Glance: Description

1. In an **objective description**, use direct, practical language and usually appeal mainly to the sense of sight.
2. In a subjective or an **emotional description**, appeal to the reader's feelings, especially through the use of images of sight, sound, smell, taste, and touch.
3. Use specific and concrete words if appropriate.
4. Be sure that readers can answer the following questions:

   What is the subject of this description?
   What is the dominant impression?
   What is the situation?
   What is the order of details—time, space, or both?
   What details support the dominant impression?

5. Use CLUESS for revision and COPS for editing. See pages 21–24 for guidance.

7

Exemplification:
Writing with Examples

～ Writing Paragraphs of Exemplification

Exemplification means using examples to explain, convince, or amuse. Lending interest and information to writing, exemplification is one of the most common and effective ways of developing ideas. Examples may be developed in a sentence or more, or they may be only phrases or even single words, as in the following sentence: "Children like packaged breakfast foods, such as *Wheaties*, *Cheerios*, and *Rice Krispies*."

Characteristics of Good Examples

As supporting information, the best examples are vivid, specific, and representative. These three qualities are closely linked and, collectively, they must support the topic sentence. The **vivid** example attracts attention. Then through a memorable presentation and the use of identifying names, the example becomes **specific** to the reader. A good example must also be **representative**; that is, it must be experienced as typical so that it can be the basis for a generalization.

Finally, and most important, the connection between the example and the topic sentence must be clear. A bizarre case of cheating may be fascinating in itself (vivid and specific), but to be effective in a paragraph on "the hard work of cheating," it must also support the topic sentence. The reader should say, in effect, "That's interesting, convincing, and memorable. Though it's unusual, I can see that it's typical of what goes on."

Techniques for Finding Examples

Writing a good paragraph of exemplification begins, as always, with prewriting. The techniques you use will depend on what you are writing about. Assuming that you begin with a topic idea, one useful

87

technique is listing. Base your list on what you have read, heard, and experienced. Here is a list on the broad topic "cheating at school":

When I copied homework
Looking at a friend's test answers
A student with hand signals
Jake and his electronic system
Time for planned cheating
Those who got caught
A person who bought a research paper
Jess, who copied from me
The Internet "Cheaters" source
The two students who exchanged identities
More work than it's worth
More stress than it's worth

Connecting Examples with Purpose

Here is the final paragraph in an essay on the topic "the hard work of cheating."

Topic sentence	`Cheating students often put themselves` `under more stress than honest students.` I
Extended example	remember someone in my junior composition class who needed a research paper, so he found a source and bought one for seventy-five dollars. The first trouble was that he had to submit the work in stages: the topic, the working bibliography, the note cards, the outline, the rough draft, and the final paper. Therefore, he went to the library and started working backward. Of course, he couldn't turn in only the bib cards actually used in the paper, and next he had to make out note cards for the material he "would be" documenting, and even make out more. After having all kinds of trouble, he realized that the bought paper was of "A" quality, whereas he had been a "C" student. He went back to his source and was told he should change the sentence structure and so on to make the paper weaker. Finally he

	dropped the class after spending more time on
	his paper than I did on mine. He also suffered
Concluding sentence	more anxiety than the students who put in the
	most work on their papers.

Transitional Words

Consider using the following transitional words to improve coherence by connecting ideas with ideas, sentences with sentences, and paragraphs with paragraphs:

- **FOR EXEMPLIFICATION:** *for example, as an example, another example, for instance, such as, including, specifically, especially, in particular, to illustrate, as an illustration, that is, i.e.* (meaning that is), *e.g.* (meaning for example)

∼ Practicing Patterns of Exemplification

Exercise 1 Completing Patterns

Fill in the blanks in the following outlines to add more examples that support the topic sentences.

1. Topic sentence: Just walking through my favorite mall [or shopping center] shows me that the world is smaller than it used to be.

    I. People of different cultures (with specific examples)

    II. Foods of different cultures (with specific examples)

    III. _____

    IV. _____

2. Topic sentence: Driving to work [or school] this month and observing the behavior of other drivers have convinced me that road rage has invaded my community.

    I. A man honking his horn impatiently at an elderly driver

    II. _____

    III. _____

∿ Examining Paragraphs of Exemplification

Student Writing

Sweet and Sour Workplace

Sarah Betrue

A full-time student and a full-time worker, Sarah Betrue has a very busy life, which would go more smoothly if she did not have so many irritations. We are likely to identify with her experiences and to admire her for beginning and ending her work day in tranquility.

Every morning as I enter my workplace, I admire the vibrant colors of both the tropical fish in the aquarium and the ancient silk Chinese robes hung from the wall. But as I take the dreaded step from the dining area to the kitchen, the scenery drastically

Topic sentence changes. Stressful and frustrating situations occur daily behind the scenes at the restaurant, making it almost impossible for me to maintain a positive attitude. Consider

Example yesterday as a typical shift. The first voices I hear are the owners complaining about how filthy the restaurant looks, although the night before the other employees and I worked with Ajax for three hours scrubbing shelves and floor sinks. As the day progresses, I try to squeeze in some extra cleaning between busy times, but I find myself doing all the extra work myself. The young girls I work with think having this job is just an extension of their social lives. During lunch hour, the dining area is packed, the line for takeout has reached a ridiculous length, and two phone

Example calls are on hold. That's when Morgan decides to call her boyfriend on her cell phone. Naturally I become frustrated and proceed to speak with her. She glares at me with fire in her eyes and screams, "I've got more important things to deal with at this time!" Getting nowhere with politeness, I grab the phone from her hand and turn it off. No sooner has this crisis ended than the house phone rings again.

Example On the line is a very unhappy woman. After listening to a few colorfully disparaging descriptions of a meal she ordered, I tell her I cannot give refunds or food exchanges if her order is not returned first. She threatens to report our restaurant to newspapers and authorities, and then she tells me to do something I am physically incapable of doing and hangs up in my ear. At the end of the day I am so angry and frustrated with having to put up with such occurrences that I want to grab hold of one of the woks and whack someone upside the head. But just as I reach for the handle, I get a vision, an image of my paycheck, and I begin to relax. I leave the

Concluding restaurant with no blood on my hands, wishing
sentence everyone a wonderful evening.

Exercise 2 Discussion and Critical Thinking

1. What evidence shows that Betrue is not essentially a negative thinker?

2. What kind of order does Betrue use for her three specific supporting examples?

3. If you were one of the owners of the restaurant, how would you react to Betrue's paragraph?

Professional Writing

Colorado Springs—Every Which Way

Eric Schlosser

> *In his best-selling book* Fast Food Nation, *Eric Schlosser exposes an ignorant and largely uncaring society dependent on fast food. At the end of unsavory supply lines are rudderless cities thickly populated by fast-food chains serving up unhealthful food. One such city is Colorado Springs.*

Colorado Springs now has the feel of a city whose identity is not yet fixed. Many longtime residents strongly oppose the extremism of the newcomers, sporting bumper stickers that say, "Don't Californicate Colorado." The city is now torn between opposing visions of what America should be. Colorado Springs has twenty-eight Charismatic Christian churches and almost twice as many pawnbrokers, a Lord's Vineyard Bookstore and a First Amendment Adult Bookstore, a Christian Medical and Dental Society and a Holey Rollers Tattoo Parlor. It has a Christian summer camp whose founder, David Noebel, outlined the dangers of rock 'n' roll in his pamphlet *Communism, Hypnotism, and the Beatles.* It has a gay entertainment complex called The Hide & Seek, where the Gay Rodeo Association meets. It has a public school principal who recently disciplined a group of sixth-grade girls for reading a book on witchcraft and allegedly casting spells. The loopiness once associated with Los Angeles has come full-blown to Colorado Springs—the strange, creative energy that crops up where the future's consciously being made, where people walk the fine line separating a visionary from a total nutcase. At the start of a new century, all sorts of things seem possible there. The cultural and the physical landscapes of Colorado Springs are up for grabs.

Exercise 3 Discussion and Critical Thinking

1. Which sentence is the better topic sentence, the first or the third? Explain why.

2. Use a phrase to indicate each example that supports the idea in the third sentence in the paragraph. Notice that they appear in contrasting patterns.

3. Does he seem to favor one vision of what America should be over the other? Do you? Discuss.

4. How does the last sentence function as part of the paragraph structure?

5. Discuss a city or a part of any community you are familiar with that is torn between opposing views of what America should be. Give some examples of establishments with implied contrasting values.

Dropping Way Out

David Levine

> *Every day, three thousand students give up on high school—for*
> *good. They push open the doors and walk out. They turn their*
> *backs on school. Drop out, way out. Here we have one of numer-*
> *ous examples of dropout experiences discussed by freelance au-*
> *thor David Levine in his essay "I'm Outta Here."*

Think about it. In some ways it seems perfect. Quit school.
Just say No—no more pressure, no more stupid rules, no more
deadlines, no more uncaring teachers, no more snobby, clique-
conscious peers. Nearly every high school student has imagined
what it would be like. Beth Kierny did more than imagine. A
few months into her senior year at Columbia High School in
East Greenbush, New York, she dropped out of school. Beth is a
shy eighteen-year-old with dark, curly hair who hated getting
up early for classes. She thought it would be great. She'd just get
a job, sleep in later, work at some cool place instead of sitting in
boring classes, and lead an easier, more interesting life. But
without a diploma, Beth found it difficult to get a job. She had
to finally settle for one at the Hessmart gas station a few miles
down Route 20. Being the youngest and newest employee, she
got stuck working the worst shifts. Often she had to get up even
earlier than she had to for school—sometimes she had to be *at*
work by 7:00 a.m. Or she'd have to work the midnight shift,
which was scary because one never knew if the place might get
held up. Or she'd have to work weekends, when her friends
were all out partying. The money was terrible—at minimum
wage she cleared maybe $90 a week—and she couldn't afford a
car, so she had to take cabs to and from work, which cost almost ten bucks a day. That didn't leave much for her share of
the $425 a month in rent on [the] small apartment behind the
Burger King.

Exercise 4 Discussion and Critical Thinking

1. In your own words, state the subject and the focus of this
   paragraph.

2. Does Levine use one example or many examples? Why?

3. What are the main narrative points in the example?

Situation:

Conflict:

Struggle:

Outcome:

Meaning:

4. Does this example correspond to what you know from your observations about those dropping out of school? Therefore, does the example work well? Explain.

∿ Topics for Paragraphs of Exemplification

Most of these topics can also be used for short essays.

Reading-Based Writing Topics

See Chapter 3 for instruction and examples for writing summaries, reactions, and two-part responses (separate paragraphs of summary and reaction). Use quotations and references. Credit source(s).

"Dropping Way Out"

1. Write an evaluation of this paragraph in which you discuss how typical Beth Kierny is of students who drop out of high school. Compare Kierny with a person or persons you have known who have also dropped out of school to enter the world of work. Give Levine credit for the ideas you borrow as you provide your own examples, pointing out their similarity or dissimilarity to the account of Beth Kierny.

General Topics

2. Write a paragraph or an essay about a town that seems to project different sets of values as it exhibits contradictory features such as institutions, stores, products, services, residents, and individual behavior. Rows of strip malls in your own or nearby communities may be especially rich locations for examples. For a helpful model of form on a similar topic, review "Colorado Springs—Every Which Way" on page 92.

3. Use examples to write a statement on how you have experienced and dealt with irritations at school, at home, at work, in a neighborhood, in theaters during a movie, in restaurants, on airplanes, on subways, on trains, on streets, or on highways. For a useful model on a similar topic, review "Sweet and Sour Workplace" on page 90.

4. Make a judgmental statement about a social issue you believe in strongly and then use an example or examples to illustrate your point. Some possible topics include the following:

    a. The price of groceries is too high.
    b. Professional athletes are paid too much.
    c. A person buying a new car may get a lemon.
    d. Drivers sometimes openly ignore the laws on a selective basis.
    e. Politicians should be watched.

Cross-Curricular Topics

5. Use examples to develop a generalization you make about one of these groups:

    a. Civil rights leaders
    b. Healthful foods
    c. Worthwhile exercises
    d. Influential artists (musicians, painters, composers, writers)
    e. Good parents
    f. Good coaches

6. Reports: Focus on one or more examples as representative of a much larger group; for example, a focused discussion of one work of art in a museum grouping of pieces by style or a study of a particular typical student in a class visit for an education class.

Career-Related Topic

7. Use specific examples to support or argue against one of the following statements as applied to business or work:

   a. It's not what you know, it's who you know.
   b. Don't burn your bridges.
   c. Like Lego, business is a matter of connections.
   d. The customer is always right.
   e. If you take care of the pennies, the dollars will take care of themselves.
   f. A kind word turns away wrath.

Writer's Guidelines at a Glance: Exemplification

1. Use examples to explain, convince, or amuse.
2. Use examples that are vivid, specific, and representative.

   - Vivid examples attract attention.
   - Specific examples are identifiable.
   - Representative examples are typical and therefore the basis for generalizations.

3. Tie your examples clearly to your topic sentence.
4. Draw your examples from what you have read, heard, and experienced.
5. Brainstorm a list of possible examples before you write.
6. Use CLUESS for revision and COPS for editing. See pages 21–24 for guidance.

8

Analysis by Division: Examining the Parts

〜 Writing Paragraphs of Analysis by Division

Being able to analyze is the key to learning, performing, and teaching. If you need to explain how something works or exists as a unit, you will write an analysis by division. You will break down a unit (your subject) into its parts and explain how each part functions in relation to the operation or existence of the whole. The most important word here is *unit*. You begin with something that can stand alone or can be regarded separately. Here are some examples of topics, or general subjects, as units that can be divided into traits, characteristics, or other parts in different contexts by applying a specific principle (your focus):

- **Personal:** a relationship, love, a parent, a neighbor, friend (traits)
- **Cross-Curricular:** a musical composition, a prepared food, an organism, a government
- **Career-Related:** a job description, an employee evaluation, a product, a service, a company

Procedure

The following procedure will guide you in writing an analysis by division. Move from subject to principle, to division, to relationship:

1. Begin with something that is a unit.
2. State the principle by which the unit functions or exists (your focus).
3. Divide the unit into parts according to that principle.
4. Discuss each of the parts in relation to the unit.

98

You might apply that procedure to evaluating a restaurant in the following way:

1. Unit	Restaurant review
2. Principle of function	Overall quality
3. Parts based on the principle	Ambiance (atmosphere), food, service
4. Discussion	Each part in relation to the quality of a dining experience

Organization

In a paragraph or an essay of analysis by division, the main parts are likely to be the main points of your outline or main extensions of your cluster. If they are anything else, reconsider your organization.

A basic outline of analysis by division might look like this:

Thesis: In judging this restaurant, one should consider these aspects.

   I. Ambiance
  II. Food
 III. Service

Sequence of Parts

The order in which you discuss the parts will vary according to the nature of the unit and the way in which you view it. Here are some possible sequences for organizing the parts of a unit.

- **Time:** The sequence of the parts in your paragraph can be based on time if you are dealing with something that functions on its own, such as a heart, with the parts presented in relation to stages of the function).
- **Space:** If your unit is a visual object, especially if, like a statue, it does nothing by itself, you may discuss the parts in relation to space.
- **Emphasis:** Because the most emphatic part of any piece of writing is the end (the second most emphatic point is the beginning), consider placing the most significant part of the unit at the end.

Transitional Words

Consider using the following transitional words to improve coherence by connecting ideas with ideas, sentences with sentences, and paragraphs with paragraphs:

- **FOR ANALYSIS BY DIVISION: Time or numbering:** *first, second, third, another, last, finally, soon, later, currently, before, along with, another part (section, component)*

- **Space:** *above, below, to the left, to the right, near, beyond, under, next to, in the background, split, divide*

- **Emphasis:** *most important, equally important, central to the, to this end, as a result, taken collectively, with this purpose in mind, working with the, in fact, of course, above all, most of all, especially, primarily, without question*

⁓ Practicing Patterns of Analysis by Division

Exercise 1 Completing Patterns

Fill in the blanks in the following outlines to complete each analysis by division.

1. Unit: Federal government

   Principle: Division of power

   Parts based on the principle:

   I. Executive

   II. _____

   III. _____

2. Unit: Good boss

   Principle: Effectiveness in leading a workforce

Parts based on the principle:

I. Fair

II. _____

III. _____

IV. _____

Examining Paragraphs
of Analysis by Division

Student Writing

More Than Ordinary

Nancy Samuels

Faced with writing on the topic of "an example of a hero, with a discussion of the hero's traits [analysis by division]," Nancy Samuels didn't have to go to the library. Right in her household she found her subject—her mother. She writes about an ordinary person who faced a difficult challenge and succeeded in a situation in which others gave up.

Topic sentence	My mother is the best example of a hero I can think of. No one will read about her in a
Unit: hero	book about heroes, but in her small circle of friends, no one doubts her heroism. Certainly
Principle: strength	my younger brother doesn't. He is the special beneficiary of the strength of her heroism. He was in an accident when he was five years old, and the doctor told us that he would never walk again. My mother listened respectfully, but she didn't believe him. She
I. Part one: Optimism	had optimism. She went to another doctor and then another. Finally she found one who prescribed exercises. She worked with my brother for three years. Day after dismal
II. Part two: Perseverance	day, she showed perseverance. It wasn't just her working with him that helped my brother.

III. Part three: It was her raw <u>courage</u> in the face of
    Courage   failure. My brother worked with her. They
both had courage. We other family members
didn't. To us my brother and mother were
acting like a couple of blind fools. We
thought my mother especially, the leader, was
in prolonged denial. But in three years my
brother was walking. He won't be an athlete;
nevertheless, he gets around. We're proud of
him, but we know—and he knows—that without
Mother he would never have walked. Of course,
she's not a miracle worker. Most of the time,
doctors are right, and some injured people
can never walk. But the ones like my brother,
who somewhere have that hidden ability, need

Concluding   that special someone like my mother. She's
  sentence   more than ordinary. <u>She's a hero.</u>

Exercise 2 Discussion and Critical Thinking

1. What are the main traits of Samuels's heroic mother?

2. Is she a miracle worker? Why or why not?

3. Will her kind of strength always succeed? Explain.

4. Would she have been considered heroic if she had not succeeded in helping her son?

Professional Writing

Golden Oldies

Jerry Bratcher

Freelance writer Jerry Bratcher reflects on one of our treasured shared experiences. He reminds us that all the songs we call "golden oldies" have common characteristics, and we note that his discussion of those characteristics is an analysis by division.

Radio stations have made golden oldies their entire program. Television infomercials have beckoned those from a particular oldie period to listen to and buy CD collections. *Golden oldies* has become a term with components familiar to all of us. Anyone can love the songs, but only listeners who were around to hear them first can truly cherish all their dimensions. Golden oldies are the songs that resonate in our memories. Merely hearing one triggers a series of related emotions and recollections, which is what makes them golden. Not all songs can be both golden and oldie. *Oldie* means it must have originated in a clearly defined historical past, probably more than ten years ago. The person who hears an oldie on the radio is reminded of the historical time of its origin; thus, the oldie will be suggestive of what was going on culturally. Though that message need not be profound, somehow, in music, style, and lyrics the golden oldie will reveal its context. More important for the individual listener, the golden oldie must have emerged at a key time in his or her life, usually in the adolescent to early adulthood range, a time of acute emotions and restless hormones. Additionally, for an oldie to be truly golden, a poignant response to the song must be shared with others of its host generation. Thus, a song treasured by only two people might be a sentimental favorite, but if it is not sanctioned by the media industry and millions of people, that's all it is. If you are not old enough to cherish a golden oldie, just wait around. Hum, chant, whistle, tap your toe, or shake your booty patiently. You probably have dozens of golden oldies in the making. A few words of warning: Your descendents not yet born may someday scorn the tunes you treasure.

Exercise 3 Discussion and Critical Thinking

Complete the following pattern:

Subject: Golden oldie

Principle of division: Components for a definition according to the common use of the term

Parts (components):

1. Historical origin: ten or more years old

2. Revealing of _____

3. Personal _____

4. Must be a shared _____

Who Are Our Heroes?

Ponchitta Pierce

> *Taken from an essay of the same name by journalist Ponchitta Pierce, this paragraph defines a personal hero by using analysis by division and supporting it with specific examples.*

The poet Maya Angelou, 67—whose works include the autobiography *I Know Why the Caged Bird Sings* and "On the Pulse of Morning," the poem she read at President Clinton's inauguration—also doesn't use the word "hero." She prefers the term "hero/shero," because "hero" too often is thought of as male. "Young women and young men need to know that there are women who give encouragement and succor, nourishment and insight," explained Angelou. "A hero/shero encourages people to see the good inside themselves and to expand it." Angelou lists Eleanor Roosevelt, the author Pearl S. Buck and the abolitionist Frederick Douglass among her heroes. "They confronted societies that did not believe in their ideas and faced hostile adversaries," she said. "At times they were angry. Anger is very good—but I have not seen any case where any of them became bitter." We can develop the heroic in ourselves, Angelou continued, by seeking to do right by others. "Are you concerned about the poor, the lonely and the ill?" she asked. "Do you follow your concern with action? I try to act as I would want my hero-shero to act. I want to display courtesy, courage, patience and strength all the time. Now, I blow it 84 times a day. But I'm trying."

Exercise 4 Discussion and Critical Thinking

1. Why does Maya Angelou use the term *hero/shero*?

2. Do you like her new word or is it unnecessary?

3. On the first line below, write the name of a hero/shero, either an ordinary person you know or have known or a famous person from history or current times. Then, for the Roman-numeral headings, write the four qualities listed by Maya Angelou, or others that are similar.

   Unit (as person):

   _____

   Parts (as qualities):

   I. _____

   II. _____

   III. _____

   IV. _____

～ Topics for Paragraphs of Analysis by Division

Most of these topics can also be used for short essays.

Reading-Based Writing Topics

See Chapter 3 for instruction and examples for writing summaries, reactions, and two-part responses (separate paragraphs of summary and reaction). Use quotations and references. Credit source(s).

"More Than Ordinary"

1. Write a paragraph in which you disagree with Samuels's idea that an ordinary person can be a hero and that to regard an ordinary person as a hero is to cheapen the word. Give examples of heroes who have the stature that is part of your own definition. Use references and quotations as you refer to the situation and the traits of the subject in this paragraph.

"Golden Oldies"

2. Write an analysis by division paragraph in which you look back on your memorable experiences in listening to songs and discuss your favorite golden oldie according to the parts presented by Bratcher: when it originated, what it reveals about the culture of that time, and how the oldie touched your life and, perhaps, the lives of others. Refer to the paragraph and use quotations.

"Who Are Our Heroes?"

3. Using Maya Angelou's definition with its parts or a slight modification of its parts as a framework, write about a well-known person from history or current times you regard as a hero. Refer to the paragraph and use quotations.

4. Adapt Angelou's definition so that it can be applied to an ordinary person who struggles and distinguishes him- or herself, perhaps only within the family. Then use that definition in discussing an example from your experience.

General Topics

5. Write about an ordinary person who has struggled mightily and deserves the title *hero*. Structure your piece around the person's achievements and traits, especially the traits. For a useful model, review "More Than Ordinary" on page 101.

6. In a paragraph of analysis by division, discuss the qualities that make someone or something successful or praiseworthy. Begin with a topic sentence such as this (modify it later to make it less mechanical): "[_____]'s success can be attributed to three [or four] qualities." The qualities would, of

course, become the main parts of your outline. Select one of these subjects:

a. A specific performer (a singer, a dancer, an actor, a musician)
b. A team, a company, a school, a class, an organization
c. A movie, a television program, a music video, a video game
d. A family, a marriage, a relationship, a club

7. Discuss how a physical object works, perhaps a part of the body (heart, ear, lungs), a part of a car (carburetor, water pump), or an object (a CD player, a stapler, a pencil sharpener, a hair dryer).

8. Write a restaurant review in which you discuss an eating place you are familiar with (fast food, campus cafeteria, restaurant). Use ambiance (atmosphere), service, and food as parts of your analysis by division. Name the place, narrate your visit, describe the particulars. See the first page of this chapter for guidance on this topic.

Cross-Curricular Topic

9. Consider the units of material in a class you are taking or have taken. Each unit has its parts: a musical composition in a music-appreciation class, a short story in an English class, an organ such as a heart in a biology class, a government in a political-science class, a management team in a business class, a family in a sociology class, a painting in an art-history class, a teacher or student in an education class, and so on. Select one unit, consult your textbook(s), talk to your instructor(s), and follow the procedure for writing an analysis by division. Credit your sources, and use quotation marks around material you borrow.

Career-Related Topics

10. Write an analysis by division about a job description, a product, a company, or a service.

11. Explain how each of several qualities of a specific person— intelligence, sincerity, knowledgeability, communication skills, manner, attitude, appearance—makes that individual an effective salesperson, manager, or employee.

Writer's Guidelines at a Glance:
Analysis by Division

1. Follow the procedure discussed in this chapter from (step 1) unit to (step 2) principle to (step 3) parts to (step 4) discussion.
2. Write a strong topic sentence to unify your writing.
3. Present the parts in a way that promotes order. Consider time, space, and emphasis.
4. Emphasize how the parts function in relation to the operation of the whole unit.
5. Your basic outline will probably look like this:

    I. Part 1
   II. Part 2
  III. Part 3

6. Use CLUESS for revision and COPS for editing. See pages 21–24 for guidance.

9

Process Analysis:
Writing About Doing

～ Writing Paragraphs of Process Analysis

If you have any doubt about how frequently we use process analysis, just think about how many times you have heard people say, "How do you do it?" or "How is [was] it done?" Even when you are not hearing those questions, you are posing them yourself when you need to make something, cook a meal, assemble an item, take some medicine, repair your car, or figure out what happened. In your college classes, you may have to discover how osmosis occurs, how a rock changes form, how a mountain was formed, how a battle was won, or how a bill goes through the legislature.

If you need to explain how to do something or how something was (is) done, you will write a paper of **process analysis**. You will break down your topic into stages, explaining each so that your reader can duplicate or understand the process.

Two Types of Process Analysis:
Directive and Informative

The questions "How do I do it?" and "How is (was) it done?" will lead you into two different types of process analysis—directive and informative.

Directive process analysis explains how to do something. As the name suggests, it gives directions and gives the reader instructions. It says, for example, "Read me, and you can bake a pie [tune up your car, solve a math problem, write an essay, take some medicine]." Because it is presented directly to the reader, it usually addresses the reader as "you," or it implies the "you" by saying something such as "First [you] purchase a large, fat wombat, and then [you]. . . ." In the same way, this textbook addresses you or implies "you" because it is a long how-to-do-it (directive process analysis) statement.

Informative process analysis explains how something was (is) done by giving data (information). Whereas the directive process analysis tells you what to do in the future, the informative process analysis tells you what has occurred or what is occurring. If it is something in nature, such as the formation of a mountain, you can read and understand the process by which it emerged. In this type of process analysis, you do not tell the reader what to do; therefore, you do not use the words *you* or *your*.

Working with Stages

Preparation

In the first stage of writing directive process analysis, list the materials or equipment needed for the process and discuss the necessary setup arrangements. For some topics, this stage will also provide technical terms and definitions. The degree to which this stage is detailed will depend on both the subject itself and the expected knowledge and experience of the projected audience.

Informative process analysis may begin with background or context rather than with preparation. For example, a statement explaining how mountains form might begin with a description of a flat portion of the earth made up of plates that are arranged like a jigsaw puzzle.

Steps

The actual process will be presented here. Each step must be explained clearly and directly, and it must be phrased to accommodate the audience. The language, especially in directive process analysis, is likely to be simple and concise; however, avoid dropping words such as *and, a, an, the,* and *of,* thereby lapsing into "recipe language." In directive process analysis the steps may be accompanied by explanations about why certain procedures are necessary and how not following directions carefully can lead to trouble. In informative process analysis the steps should appear in a logical progression within a sequence.

Order

The order will usually be chronological (time-based) in some sense.

Transitional Words

Consider using the following transitional words to improve coherence by connecting ideas with ideas, sentences with sentences, and paragraphs with paragraphs:

- **FOR PROCESS ANALYSIS:** *first, second, third, then, soon, now, next, finally, at last, therefore, consequently,* and— especially for informative process analysis—words used to show the passage of time, such as hours, days of the week, and so on.

⁓ Basic Forms

Consider using this form for directive process analysis (with topics such as how to cook something or how to fix something).

    I. Preparation
       A.
       B.
       C.
   II. Steps
       A.
       B.
       C.
       D.

Consider using this form for informative process analysis (with topics such as how a volcano functions or how a battle was won).

    I. Background or context
       A.
       B.
       C.
   II. Change or development (narrative)
       A.
       B.
       C.
       D.

〜 Practicing Patterns of Process Analysis

Underlying a process analysis is a definite pattern. In some presentations, such as directions with merchandise to be assembled, the content reads as mechanically as an outline, and no reader objects. The same can be said of most recipes. In other presentations, such as your typical college assignments, the pattern is submerged in flowing discussion. The directions or information must be included, but the writing should be well developed and interesting. Regardless of the form you use or the audience you anticipate, keep in mind that in process analysis the pattern provides a foundation for the content.

Exercise 1 Completing Patterns

A. Using directive process analysis, fill in the blanks in the following outline for replacing a flat tire with a spare. Work in a group if possible.

    I. Preparation

        A. Park car.

        B. _____

        C. Obtain car jack.

        D. _____

        E. _____

    II. Steps

        A. Remove hub cap (if applicable).

        B. Loosen lug nuts a bit.

        C. _____

        D. _____

        E. Remove wheel with flat tire.

        F. _____

        G. _____

        H. Release jack pressure.

        I. _____

B. *Using informative process analysis, fill in the blanks in the following outline for an explanation of how a watermelon seed grows into a plant and produces a watermelon. Work in a group if possible.*

I. Background (what happens before the sprouting)

   A. Seed planted in cultivated land

   B. _____

   C. Receives heat (from sun)

II. Sequence (becomes plant and produces fruit)

   A. Sprouts

   B. _____

   C. Responds to sunlight and air

   D. _____

   E. _____

   F. Flower pollinated

   G. _____

～ Examining Paragraphs of Process Analysis

Student Writing

Pupusas: Salvadoran Delight

Patty Serrano

We all have at least one kind of food that reminds us of childhood, something that has filled our bellies in times of hunger and perhaps comforted our minds in times of stress. For Patty Serrano, a community college student living at home, that special dish is pupusas. In El Salvador these are a favorite item in homes and restaurants and at roadside stands. In Southern California, they are available in little restaurants called pupusarias.

                Every time my mom decides to make

Topic sentence pupusas, we jump for joy. A pupusa contains
only a few ingredients, and it may sound easy
to make, but really good ones must be made by

experienced hands. My mom is an expert,
having learned as a child from her mother in

Preparation   El Salvador. All the ingredients are chosen
fresh. The meat, either pork or beef, can be
bought prepared, but my mom chooses to

Step 1   prepare it herself. The meat, which is called
"carnitas," is ground and cooked with
tomatoes and spices. The cheese—she uses a
white Jalisco—has to be stringy because that
kind gives pupusas a very good taste,
appearance, and texture. Then comes the

Step 2   preparation of the "masa," or cornmeal. It
has to be soft but not so soft that it falls
apart in the making and handling. All of this
is done while the "comal," or skillet, is

Step 3   being heated. She then grabs a chunk of masa
and forms it into a tortilla like a magician
turning a ball into a thin pancake. Next she

Step 4   grabs small chunks of meat and cheese and
Step 5   places them in the middle of the tortilla.
The tortilla is folded in half and formed

Step 6   again. After placing the pupusa into the
sizzling skillet with one hand, she is
already starting another pupusa. It is
amazing how she does two things at the same

Step 7   time. She turns the pupusas over and over
again until she is sure that they are done.
We watch, mouths open, plates empty. In my
family it is a tradition that I get the first
pupusa because I like them so much. I love
opening the hot pupusas, smelling the aroma,
and seeing the stringy cheese stretching in
the middle. I am as discriminating as a wine
taster. But I never eat a pupusa without
"curtido," chopped cabbage with jalapeño.
Those items balance the richness of the other

Concluding sentences	ingredients. <u>I could eat Mom's pupusas forever. I guess it has something to do with the way she makes them, with magical, experienced, loving hands.</u>

Exercise 2 Discussion and Critical Thinking

1. Is this writing mainly informative or directive—or is it actually both? Explain.

2. Is Serrano's intended audience those who want to learn how to make *pupusas* or those who want to read about her love of *pupusas* as *pupusas* are related to her mother, or both?

3. What concrete details give this process analysis the feel of reality, meaning that Serrano knows what she is writing about?

Making Faces

Seham Hemmat

By evening, Seham Hemmat is a community college student. By day, she is an employee of a mall specialty store where, to use her words, she does "face detail work." She rewrote this paragraph of process analysis six times, twice reading it aloud to her peer group and listening to their suggestions (especially those from the two male members) before she was satisfied with the content and tone. Her word choice suggests a somewhat humorous view of work she takes seriously but not too seriously.

The Face Place, a trendy mall store, is where I work. Making faces is what I do. I don't mean sticking out my tongue; I mean reworking the faces of women who want a new or fresh look. When I get through, if I've done a good job, you can't tell if my subject **Topic** is wearing makeup or not. <u>If you'd like to do</u> **sentence** <u>what I do, just follow these directions.</u>

Imagine you have a client. Her name is Donna. **Preparation** <u>Check her out</u> for skin complexion, skin condition, size of eyes, kind of eyebrows, and lip shape. Then <u>go to the supply room and</u> <u>select</u> the <u>items</u> you need for the faceover, including a cleanser and toner with added **Step 1** moisturizers. <u>Put them on a tray by your</u> <u>brushes and other tools and basic supplies.</u> <u>Begin by stripping off her old makeup</u> with a few cotton balls and cleanser. Donna's skin is a combination of conditions. Her forehead, nose, and chin are oily, and her cheeks are **Step 2** dry. <u>Scrub her down</u> with Tea Tree, my favorite facial cleanser from a product line that is not tested on animals. Scour the oil **Step 3** slicks extra. Then <u>slather on</u> some <u>Tea Tree</u> <u>toner</u> to close her pores so that the dirt **Step 4** doesn't go back in. <u>Add</u> a <u>very light</u> <u>moisturizer</u> such as one called Elderflower **Step 5** Gel. Donna has a pale complexion. <u>Put on a</u> <u>coat of 01 foundation</u>, the fairest in the shop, which evens out her skin tone. Next, **Step 6** with a big face brush, <u>dust on a layer of 01</u> <u>powder</u> to give her a smooth, dry look. Now Donna, who's watching in a mirror, speaks up to say she wants her eyebrows brushed and lightened just a bit. She has dark eyebrows and eyelashes that won't require much mascara

Step 7   or eyebrow pencil. So use gel to fix the
eyebrows in place while you trim, shape, and
pencil them. Move downward on the face, going

Step 8   next to her eyes. Use brown mascara to curl
her already dark lashes. With your blusher

Step 9   brush, dab some peach rose blush on her

Step 10   cheeks and blend it in. Line her lips with
bronze sand lip liner pencil and fill in the
rest with rouge mauve lipstick. Swing Donna
around to the big lighted mirror. Watch her
pucker her lips, squint her eyes, flirt with
herself. See her smile. Now you pocket the

Concluding   tip. Feel good. You've just given a woman a

sentence   new face, and she's out to conquer the world.

Exercise 3   Discussion and Critical Thinking

1. Is this paragraph of process analysis mainly directive or informative? Or is it both? Discuss.

2. How does Hemmat take her paragraph beyond a list of mechanical directions?

3. In addition to using chronological order (time), what other order does she use briefly and why does she do so?

4. What word choice may have come from suggestions offered by the males in her discussion group?

Professional Writing

How to Sharpen a Knife

Florence H. Pettit

> *The simplest tasks are often the most poorly done because we as-*
> *sume that we know how to do them and do not seek instruction.*
> *Florence H. Pettit explains here how to sharpen a knife properly,*
> *and what we learn reminds us that we could probably take*
> *lessons on performing any number of everyday chores.*

If you have never done any whittling or wood carving before, the first skill to learn is how to sharpen your knife. You
may be surprised to learn that even a brand-new knife needs
sharpening. Knives are never sold honed (finely sharpened),
although some gouges and chisels are. It is essential to learn the
firm stroke on the stone that will keep your blades sharp. The
sharpening stone must be fixed in place on the table, so that it
will not move around. You can do this by placing a rubber inner
tube or a thin piece of foam rubber under it. Or you can tack
four strips of wood, if you have a rough worktable, to frame the
stone and hold it in place. Put a generous puddle of oil on the
stone—this will soon disappear into the surface of a new stone,
and you will need to keep adding more oil. Press the knife blade
flat against the stone in the puddle of oil, using your index finger. Whichever way the cutting edge of the knife faces is the
side of the blade that should get a little more pressure. Move
the blade around three or four times in a narrow oval about the
size of your fingernail, going *counterclockwise* when the sharp
edge is facing right. Now turn the blade over in the same spot
on the stone, press hard, and move it around the small oval
clockwise, with more pressure on the cutting edge that faces
left. Repeat the ovals, flipping the knife blade over six or seven
times, and applying lighter pressure to the blade the last two
times. Wipe the blade clean with a piece of rag or tissue and rub
it flat on the piece of leather strop at least twice on each side.
Stroke *away* from the cutting edge to remove the little burr of
metal that may be left on the blade.

Exercise 4 Discussion and Critical Thinking

1. What type of process analysis (informative or directive) is used?

2. To what type of audience (well informed, moderately informed, or poorly informed on the topic) does Pettit direct this selection?

3. What is the prevailing tone (objective, humorous, reverent, argumentative, cautionary, playful, ironic, ridiculing) of this selection?

4. Make an X at the point at which the preparation (materials, setup, explaining words, and so on) ends and the steps begin.

5. Write numbers in the margin to indicate the steps or stages in the process.

6. Circle any transitional words indicating time or other progression (*first, second, then, soon, now, next, after, before, when, finally, at last, therefore, consequently,* and—especially for the informative process analysis—words used to show the passage of time, such as hours, days of the week, and so on).

7. Is Pettit trying to inform or to persuade?

◯ Topics for Paragraphs of Process Analysis

Most of these topics can also be used for short essays.

Reading-Based Writing Topic

See Chapter 3 for instruction and examples for writing summaries, reactions, and two-part responses (separate paragraphs of summary and reaction). Use quotations and references. Credit source(s).

"Making Faces"

1. Evaluate this paragraph in terms of the principles of writing a directive process analysis. Include comments on diction. The introduction indicated that Hemmat may have used some terms suggested by male members of her discussion group. If so, what words might they be? Explain how those words brighten the paragraph or detract from its message?

General Topics

2. Write about how a favorite meal of yours is prepared by someone you know. Personalize this by putting it in the context of a household, perhaps even a special occasion such as a holiday or an ethnic celebration. For a model paragraph on a similar topic, review "*Pupusas:* Salvadoran Delight" on page 113.
3. Write a process analysis on how to perform a simple task such as cleaning a shower or an oven, snow-sealing boots, defrosting a freezer, or waxing a car. For a helpful model on a similar topic, review "How to Sharpen a Knife" on page 118.
4. Most of the topics in the following list are directive as they are phrased. However, each can be transformed into a how-it-was-done informative topic by personalizing it and explaining stage by stage how you, someone else, or a group did something. For example, you could write either a directive process analysis about how to deal with an obnoxious person or an informative process analysis about how you or someone else dealt with an obnoxious person. Keep in mind that the two types of process analysis are often blended, especially in the personal approach.

Many of the following topics will be more interesting to you and your readers if they are personalized.

Select one of the following topics and write a process-analysis paragraph about it. Most of the topics require some narrowing to be treated in a paragraph. For example, writing about playing baseball is too broad; writing about how to throw a curve ball may be manageable.

a. How to pass a test for a driver's license
b. How to get a job at (   )_____
c. How to eat or prepare a food _____
d. How to teach a dog to behave or perform a trick
e. How to repair or assemble (   ) _____
f. How to end a relationship without hurting someone's feelings

Cross-Curricular Topics

5. Write a paragraph about a procedure you follow in your college work in a science (chemistry, biology, geology) lab. You may explain how to analyze a rock, how to dissect something, how to operate something, or how to perform an experiment.
6. Write a paragraph about how to do something in an activity or a performance class, such as drama, physical education, art, or music.

Career-Related Topics

7. Explain how to display, package, sell, or demonstrate a product.
8. Explain how to perform a service or how to repair or install a product.
9. Explain the procedure for operating a machine, a computer, a piece of equipment, or another device.
10. Explain how to manufacture, construct, or cook something.

Writer's Guidelines at a Glance: Process Analysis

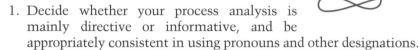

1. Decide whether your process analysis is mainly directive or informative, and be appropriately consistent in using pronouns and other designations.

   - For the directive analysis, use the second person, addressing the reader as *you*. The *you* may be understood, even if it is not written.
   - For the informative analysis:

     a. Use the first person, speaking as *I* or *we*
     b. Or use the third person, speaking about the subject as *he, she, it,* or *they,* or by name.

2. Consider using these basic forms.

Directive	Informative
I. Preparation	I. Background or context
A.	A.
B.	B.
II. Steps	II. Change or development
A.	A.
B.	B.
C.	C.

3. In explaining the stages and using technical terms, take into account whether your audience will be mainly well informed, moderately informed, or poorly informed.
4. Use transitional words indicating time or other progression (such as *first, second, then, soon, now, next, after, before, when, finally, at last, therefore, consequently,* and—especially for the informative process analysis—words that show passage of time, such as hours, days of the week, and so on).
5. Avoid recipe language by not dropping *the, a, an,* or *of.*
6. Use CLUESS for revision and COPS for editing. See pages 21–24 for guidance.

10

Cause and Effect: Determining Reasons and Outcomes

∿ Writing Paragraphs of Cause and Effect

Cause-and-effect relationships are common in our daily lives. A single situation may raise questions about both causes and effects:

> *The car won't start.*
> *Why?* (cause)
> *What now?* (effect)

In a paragraph, you will probably concentrate on either causes or effects, although you may mention both of them. Because you cannot write about all causes or all effects, you should try to identify and develop the most important ones. Consider that some causes are immediate, others remote; some visible, others hidden. Any one or a group of causes can be the most important. The effects of an event can also be complicated. Some may be immediate, others long range. The sequence of events is not necessarily related to causation. For example, *B* (inflation) may follow *A* (the election of a president), but that sequence does not mean that *A* caused *B*.

Organizing Cause and Effect

One useful approach to developing a cause-and-effect analysis is **listing**. In the middle of the page write down the event, situation, or trend you are concerned about. Then, on the left side of the page list the causes and on the right side list the effects. Looking at the two lists, determine the better side (causes or effects) for your study.

123

Causes	Event, Situation, or Trend	Effects
Bad habits		Financial problems
In-law problems		Liberation
Religious differences		Financial success
Career decision		Safety
Personal abuse	*Divorce*	New relationships
Infidelity		Social adjustment
Sexual incompatibility		Vocational choice
Politics		Problems for children
Money		Independence

First, evaluate the items on your list. Keep in mind that one cause, such as personal abuse, may have its own (remote, hidden, or underlying) cause or partial cause: frustration over job loss, mental-health problems, drug addiction, bad parenting, or weak character. In single paragraphs, one usually deals with immediate causes, such as in-law problems, money, and personal abuse. (These same principles can be applied to effects.)

After you have evaluated the items on your list, choose two or three of the most important causes or effects and proceed.

The causes could be incorporated into a preliminary topic sentence and then developed in an outline.

> *Preliminary topic sentence:* The main causes of my divorce were in-law problems, money, and personal abuse.

I. In-law problems
   A. Helped too much
   B. Expected too much
II. Money
   A. Poor management
   B. Low-paying job
III. Personal abuse
   A. Verbal
   B. Physical

Your paragraph will derive its structure from either causes or effects, although both causes and effects may be mentioned. Give emphasis and continuity to your writing by repeating key words, such as *cause, reason, effect, result, consequence,* and *outcome.*

The basic structure of your paragraph may look like this:

Topic sentence
Cause (or Effect) 1
Cause (or Effect) 2
Cause (or Effect) 3

Order

The order of the causes and effects you discuss in your paper may be based on time, space, emphasis, or a combination.

Transitional Words

Consider using the following transitional words to improve coherence by connecting ideas with ideas, sentences with sentences, and paragraphs with paragraphs:

- **FOR CAUSE AND EFFECT: Cause:** *as, because, because of, due to, for, for the reason that, since, bring about, another cause, for this reason, one cause, a second cause, another cause, a final cause*

- **Effect:** *accordingly, finally, consequently, hence, so, therefore, thus, as a consequence, as a result, resulting*

∽ Practicing Patterns of Cause and Effect

Exercise 1 Completing Patterns

Fill in the blanks to complete first the causes outline and then the effects outline.

1. Causes for immigrating to the United States

   I. Desire for a better education

   II. _____

   III. _____

   IV. _____

2. Effects of getting adequate exercise

    I. Muscle tone

    II. _____

    III. _____

    IV. _____

⌒ Examining Paragraphs of Cause and Effect

Student Writing

A Divorce with Reasons

Sarah Bailey

A few years have passed, and student Sarah Bailey can look back on her divorce and sort out the causes and effects of her failed marriage. This paragraph, which focuses on three main causes, was developed through the listing and outlining shown on page 124.

I was married for almost five years. The first year was great, but each of the last four was worse than the previous one. <u>The marriage was made in carefree leisure, and the divorce</u> **I. Cause 1: In-law problems** <u>was made in a reality that just got colder and colder. Our first problem was the in-laws,</u> actually his parents; mine live in another state, and we saw them only once a year. It was nothing deliberate. His parents wanted to help, and that was the problem. They expected me to be the daughter they never had and him to be a successful businessman and homeowner. They expected too much from both of us, and **II. Cause 2: Money** we couldn't make our own choices. <u>That cause was related to another one—money.</u> Both of us had low-level jobs in industry. We were around people who were wealthy, but we couldn't buy, belong, and participate as we wanted to. Then I started getting more promotions than he. Finally, he quit his job just at the beginning of a recession, and he couldn't get another one. I told him I would be patient, but at times I was resentful that I was the only one working. As he became more

III. Cause 3: and more frustrated, he started losing his
Abuse temper with me and said things that <u>hurt my</u>
A. Personal
B. Physical <u>feelings</u>. <u>One day he hit me</u>. He said he was sorry and even cried, but I could not forgive him. We got a divorce. It took me a while before I could look back and see what the causes really were, but by then it was too late to make any changes.

Exercise 2 Discussion and Critical Thinking

1. Bailey says it took her too long to discover the causes of her divorce, so she was unable to deal with the problems. Looking at this case in speculation, would you say the problems can be found mainly in character or circumstance? Explain.

2. If Bailey had chosen to include more discussion of the effects of this divorce, what might she have mentioned?

More Than the Classroom

Richard Blaylock

Responding to an assignment on a topic organized mainly around causes and effects, Richard Blaylock chose to write about the consequences of his becoming a college student. With much trepidation, at thirty-three he had enrolled in the evening program at a local community college. The reasons for his being there were multiple, and so, surprising to him, were the results.

"We think you would benefit from our work-study program," he said to me. He wasn't my high school counselor, and I wasn't eighteen. He was the division manager, and he had just offered to pay my expenses for attending a local community college. At thirty-three, I was working for a large company in a dead-end job, dead-end because I wasn't qualified for any management positions. Naturally, I enrolled in college. More benefits than I expected were to follow. I had hardly started when the first response greeted me: my family was clearly proud. I heard my two kids in elementary school bragging about me to kids in the neighborhood. They even brought me some of their tough homework questions. My wife had lots of questions about college. We talked about taking a class together. Unlike me, she had been a good student in high school. Then I had had no interest in going on to college. Now I did, and one thing led to another. A geography class connected me with a geology class. A political-science class moved me to subscribe to the *Los Angeles Times*. I became more curious about a variety of subjects, and I felt more confident in dealing with ideas. At work my supervisors started asking me to become more involved in ongoing projects and

planning. By the time I had taken my second
English class, I was writing reports with much
more confidence and skill. Now, after
receiving a good job review and being
interviewed by my plant manager, I am in line
for a promotion that I once thought was beyond
my reach. I had expected mainly a classroom.
I found much more.

Exercise 3 Discussion and Critical Thinking

1. What is the subject and what is the focus of this paragraph?

2. Is this a paragraph mainly of causes or effects? Explain.

3. List each effect—the benefits.

4. Show how narration is used as the framework for this cause and
   effect paragraph.

   Situation:

   Conflict:

   Struggle:

   Outcome:

   Meaning:

Professional Writing

Results of Underage Drinking

Wayne D. Hoyer and Deborah J. MacInnis

In their college textbook Consumer Behavior, *Professors Wayne D.
Hoyer and Deborah J. MacInnis discuss the perils of underage
drinking as a major problem for both the individual drinkers and
society.*

Nearly 45 percent of college students have engaged in "binge drinking" (consuming more than five drinks in one sitting). Four million minors are alcoholics or problem drinkers. This often-downplayed behavior has a devastating impact on both themselves and society at large. Overuse of alcohol has been involved in 70 percent of campus violence cases, 68 percent of campus property damage cases, and 40 percent of academic failures, making it the primary discipline, emotional, and physical problem on college campuses. Alcohol is also involved in roughly half of teen highway fatalities, half of all youth suicides, and 90 percent of campus hazing deaths. Almost half of all schools polled say alcohol is the most serious problem they face. Alcohol is implicated even in the rising costs of college tuition. Now that colleges are liable for campus drinking incidents, the cost of insurance (and hence tuition) has skyrocketed. Accidents due to drinking also contribute to the high cost of automobile insurance for young consumers. To combat these problems, groups like Mothers Against Drunk Driving (MADD) and Students Against Drunk Driving (SADD) work to enact legislation to punish drinking and driving, use social disapproval to pressure students not to drink and drive, and institute programs that stress the importance of having a designated driver.

Exercise 4 Discussion and Critical Thinking

1. What is the subject and what is the specific focus of the topic sentence?

2. Underline the concluding sentence that completes the developed idea. *Hint:* The topic sentence states the problem, the development gives support for that view, and the concluding sentence gives a final response to the topic sentence.

3. Is this paragraph organized mainly around causes or effects?

4. Complete the following list to show the main effects. Add additional points if you like.

> *Topic Sentence:* Underage drinking has devastating effects on both the consumer and society at large.

   1. Campus violence _____

   2. Campus _____

   3. Academic _____

   4. Teen highway fatalities _____

   5. Youth suicides _____

   6. Campus _____

   7. Rising _____

   8. High cost of _____

   _____

   _____

5. Which of these effects pertain more to four-year colleges with mostly resident students than to colleges with mostly commuter students? Discuss.

6. What about the causes of alcohol abuse among underage drinkers? Your observations of the behavior of these underage drinkers may give you some special insights. Discuss.

∼ Topics for Paragraphs of Cause and Effect

Most of these topics can also be used for short essays.

Reading-Based Writing Topic

See Chapter 3 for instruction and examples for writing summaries, reactions, and two-part responses (separate paragraphs of summary and reaction). Use quotations and references. Credit source(s).

"Results of Underage Drinking"

1. Pick three effects of underage drinking from this paragraph and discuss them in relation to what you have specifically experienced or observed. Refer to the paragraph and use quotations. Conclude by comments on what should be done by society.

General Topics

2. Write a paragraph about the causes or effects of a divorce on someone you know, either a divorced person or a relative of a divorced person. For a useful model on a similar topic, review "A Divorce with Reasons" on page 126.
3. Write about the causes for or effects of the good marriage of a couple you know.
4. Using "More Than the Classroom" on page 128 as a model, write a paragraph about the causes and the actual or anticipated effects of your going to college.
5. Write a paragraph about the causes of crime (for one individual involved in crime), unemployment (one person who is out of work), leaving home (one person who has left home), emigrating (one person or family), poverty (one person who is poor), school dropout (one person), going to college (one who did), or the success of a product or program on television (one).
6. Write a paragraph about the effects of disease (a particular disease, perhaps on just one person), fighting (one or two people involved in a dispute), fire (a particular one), alcoholism (a certain alcoholic), getting a job (a person with a particular job), early marriage (a person who married very young), teenage parenthood (one person or a couple), or dressing a certain way (one person and his or her style).

Cross-Curricular Topic

7. From a class that you are taking or have taken, select a subject that is especially concerned with causes and effects and develop a topic. Begin by selecting an event, a situation, or a trend in the class content and make a list of the causes or effects; that procedure will almost immediately show you whether you have a topic you can discuss effectively. Class notes and text-books can provide you with more specific information. If you use textbooks or other materials, give credit to the sources. In-structors across the campus may have suggestions for studies of cause and effect. Some areas for your search include history, political science, geology, astronomy, psychology, philosophy, sociology, real estate, child development, education, fashion merchandising, psychiatric technician program, nursing, police science, fire science, physical education, and restaurant and food-service management.

Career-Related Topics

8. Discuss the effects (benefits) of a particular product or service on the business community, family life, society generally, specific groups (age, income, activities), or an individual.
9. Discuss the needs (thus the cause of development) by individuals, families, or institutions for a particular product or type of product.
10. Discuss the effects of using a certain approach, system, or philosophy in sales, human resources, or customer service.

Writer's Guidelines at a Glance: Cause and Effect

1. Have your purpose clearly in mind.
2. Be sure you have sufficient knowledge of the subject to develop it.
3. Distinguish clearly between causes and effects by using three columns. From your lists, select only the most relevant causes or effects.

Causes	Event, Situation, or Trend	Effects

4. Concentrate primarily on either causes or effects. You may refer to both causes and effects, but use only one as the framework for writing your paragraph.
5. Do not conclude that something is an effect merely because it follows something else.
6. Emphasize your main concern, cause or effect, by repeating key words such as *cause, reason, effect, result, consequence,* and *outcome.*
7. Use CLUESS for revision and COPS for editing. See pages 21–24 for guidance.

11

Comparison and Contrast: Showing Similarities and Differences

∼ Writing Paragraphs of Comparison and Contrast

Comparison and contrast is a method of showing similarities and dissimilarities between subjects. Comparison is concerned with organizing and developing points of similarity; contrast has the same function for dissimilarity. Sometimes a writing assignment may require that you cover only similarities or only dissimilarities. Occasionally, an instructor may ask you to separate one from the other. Usually, you will combine them. For convenience, the term *comparison* is often applied to both comparison and contrast because both use the same techniques and are usually combined into one operation.

Generating Topics and Working with the 4 *P*'s

Comparison and contrast is basic to your thinking. In your daily activities, you consider similarities and dissimilarities among persons, things, concepts, political leaders, doctors, friends, instructors, schools, nations, classes, movies, and so on. You naturally turn to comparison and contrast to solve problems and to make decisions in your affairs and in your writing. Because you have had so many comparative experiences, finding a topic to write about is likely to be only a matter of choosing from a great number of appealing ideas. Freewriting, brainstorming, and clustering will help you generate topics that are especially workable and appropriate for particular assignments.

135

Many college writing assignments will specify a topic or ask you to choose one from a list. Regardless of the source of your topic, the procedure for developing your ideas by comparison and contrast is the same as the procedure for developing topics of your own choosing. That procedure can be appropriately called the "4 *P's*": purpose, points, patterns, and presentation.

Purpose

Are you trying to show relationships (how things are similar and dissimilar) or to show that one side is better (ranking)? If you want to show that one actor, one movie, one writer, one president, one product, or one idea is better than another, your purpose is to persuade. You will emphasize the superiority of one side over the other in your topic sentence and in your support.

If you want to explain something about a topic by showing each subject in relation to others, then your purpose is informative. For example, you might be comparing two composers, Beethoven and Mozart. Both were musical geniuses, so you then decide it would be senseless to argue that one is superior to the other. Instead, you choose to reveal interesting information about both by showing them in relation to each other.

You may have heard people talk about puppy love and true love and now you decide to explore those two varieties as a topic for a comparative study. Your purpose would be to explain that puppy love and true love are different.

Points

Continuing with the example of two types of love, you would come up with a list of ideas, or points, that you could apply somewhat equally to the two types. From the list, you would select two or three and circle them.

(passion)
intimacy
(age of lovers)
commitment
duration
(circumstances)

Patterns

You then would need to organize your material according to the two basic patterns: subject by subject and point by point. The **subject-by-subject pattern** presents all of one side and then all of the other side.

I. Puppy love
  A. Passion
  B. Intimacy
  C. Commitment
II. True love
  A. Passion
  B. Intimacy
  C. Commitment

The **point-by-point pattern** shows the points in relation to the sides (subjects) one at a time. This is the more common pattern.

I. Passion
  A. Puppy love
    1. Consuming
    2. Intense
  B. True love
    1. Present
    2. Proportional
II. Intimacy
  A. Puppy love
    1. Lots of talking
    2. Superficial
  B. True love
    1. Good communication
      a. Feelings
      b. Ideas
    2. Deep
III. Commitment
  A. Puppy love
    1. Not tested
    2. Weak, if at all
  B. True love
    1. Proven
    2. Profound

Presentation

Here you would use your outline (or cluster list) to begin writing your paragraph. You would use appropriate explanations, details, and examples for support. See page 139 for a final draft of this topic in the point-by-point pattern.

Transitional Words

Consider using the following transitional words to improve coherence by connecting ideas with ideas, sentences with sentences, and paragraphs with paragraphs:

- **FOR COMPARISON AND CONTRAST: Comparison:** *in the same way, similarly, likewise, also, by comparison, in a like manner, as, with, as though, both, like, just as*

- **Contrast:** *but, by contrast, in contrast, despite, however, instead, nevertheless, on (to) the contrary, in spite of, still, yet, unlike, even so, rather than, otherwise*

∼ Practicing Patterns of Comparison and Contrast

Exercise 1 Practicing Patterns

Fill in the blanks in the following outlines to complete the comparisons and contrasts.

Subject-by-Subject Pattern

1. Friends: Marla and Justine

    I. Marla

        A. Appearance

        B. _____

        C. _____

II. Justine

    A. _____

    B. Personality

    C. _____

Point-by-Point Pattern

2. Two bosses: Mr. Santo and Ms. Elliott

    I. Disposition

        A. Mr. Santo

        B. Ms. Elliott

    II. Knowledge of _____

        A. _____

        B. Ms. Elliott

  III. _____

        A. Mr. Santo

        B. _____

~ Examining Paragraphs of Comparison and Contrast

Student Writing

Two Loves: Puppy and True

Jennifer Jeffries

Jennifer Jeffries considered several topics before she selected different kinds of love. Just a bit of freewriting convinced her that she had the information and interest to do a good job. In a psychology course she had recently taken, she studied the topic of love, and here she does a variation on a theory by R. J. Sternberg. She submitted a copy of Sternberg's theory with her paragraph.

        Of the several forms of love, the two opposite extremes are puppy love and true **Topic** love. If love in its fullest form has three

sentence	parts—passion, intimacy, and commitment—then puppy love and true love could be called
Point	*incomplete* and *complete*, respectively. Passion is common to both. Puppy love couldn't exist without *passion*, hence the word *puppy*—an immature animal that jumps around excitedly licking somebody's face. A
Subject A	person in <u>puppy love</u> is attracted physically to someone and is constantly aroused. A
Subject B	person in <u>true love</u> is also passionate, but the passion is proportional to other parts of love—and life. True-love passion is based on more than physical attraction, though that should not be discounted. It is with the
Point	<u>intimacy</u> factor that puppy love really begins
Subject A	to differ from true love. <u>Puppy love</u> may promote a lot of talk, but most of it can be attributed to the arousal factor. There's no closeness and depth of shared experience. But
Subject B	with <u>true love</u> there is a genuine closeness and shared concern for each other that is supportive and reassuring. That closeness usually comes from years of shared experience, which also proves commitment. And
Point	it is just that factor, the <u>commitment</u>, that
Subject A	is probably the main difference between <u>puppy love</u> and true love. The people in puppy love may talk about eternity, but their love hasn't really gotten outside the physical realm. Their love has not been tested, whereas those in true love have a proven
Subject B	commitment. <u>True love</u> has survived troubles in this imperfect world and become stronger. And it has survived because it has more than the one dimension. These considerations show that these two loves are very different,

```
though puppy love may, with time, become true
love. That possibility doesn't mean that age
necessarily corresponds with one form of
love. A person of any age can, by knowing
passion, intimacy, and commitment, experience
true love, but true love is more likely to
develop over a period of time.
```

Exercise 2 Discussion and Critical Thinking

1. Do you agree with Jeffries's decision to use the point-by-point pattern rather than the subject-by-subject one? Why or why not?

2. Jeffries says that puppy love can become true love. Can true love ever become puppy love? Discuss.

3. Jeffries implies that one is much more likely to fall out of puppy love than true love. Do you agree? Why or why not?

4. How much time is required for true love to develop? Explain.

A Summary of "The Messy Are in Denial"

Bill Walker

Bill Walker's assignment was to read "The Messy Are in Denial" by Joyce Gallagher and to write a summary that would show Walker's understanding of the main ideas.

In "The Messy Are in Denial" Joyce Gallagher explains that there are two kinds of people, the orderly and the disorderly. She discusses them according to their state of mind, behavior, and group history. As for state of mind, the disorganized people live for tomorrow. They are the daydreamers and seers. They can be creative, sometimes as "artists" and "musicians," but also "flakes" (285). The orderly, on the other hand, are practical people who put things and keep things in order. Their behavior is consistent with their state of mind. The disorderly collect all kinds of items and do not throw them away. They "run the risk of inundating themselves with their own junk" (285). The orderly are the opposite. They throw things away, clean up, and organize. They make life possible for the disorganized. The author is married to a disorganized person. She understands his nature and her purpose. Gallagher says that historically these two groups have evolved according to natural selection. She reasons that Neanderthals were too disorganized and were replaced by the better-organized *homo sapiens*, who are comparatively neat. She says drawings in anthropology books show the Neanderthals to be messy and poorly dressed. She concludes by saying she imagines that throughout history

the organized have helped the disorganized in
their daily lives.

Work Cited

Gallagher, Joyce. "The Messy Are in Denial."
Paragraphs and Essays: A Worktext with
Readings. Ed. Lee Brandon. 9th ed.
Boston: Houghton, 2005. 284-86. Print.

Exercise 3 Discussion and Critical Thinking

1. Is this paragraph of summary organized by the point-by-point or
   the subject-by-subject pattern?

2. What are the points?

3. Assuming that everyone tends to lean toward being messy or
   being neat, which one is your tendency, and where are you on
   a ten-point scale of your category, with ten being high?

4. What success would you predict for a married couple of 10s
   with opposite behavior (organized and disorganized, meaning
   neat and messy)?

5. Do you think author Joyce Gallagher is serious about what is
   stated in the last four sentences? Discuss.

6. Are you pleased with what you are or do you wish you could change? Explain.

7. Do you agree with Gallagher that the organized, or neat, make meaningful life possible for the disorganized, or messy? Explain.

Professional Writing

Blue as in Boy, *Pink as in* Girl*

Sharon S. Brehm

> *This paragraph comes from "Stereotypes, Prejudices, and Discrimination," a chapter in* Social Psychology, *a college textbook by Sharon S. Brehm. Comparing males and females, she maintains that discrimination based on gender begins at birth and never stops.*

When a baby is born, the first words uttered ring loud and clear: "It's a boy!" or "It's a girl!" In many hospitals, the newborn boy immediately is given a blue hat and the newborn girl a pink hat. The infant receives a gender-appropriate name and is showered with gender-appropriate gifts. Over the next few years, the typical boy is supplied with toy trucks, baseballs, pretend tools, guns, and chemistry sets; the typical girl is furnished with dolls, stuffed animals, pretend make-up kits, kitchen sets, and tea sets. As they enter school, many expect the boy to earn money by delivering newspapers and to enjoy math and computers, while they expect the girl to babysit and to enjoy crafts, music, and social activities. These distinctions persist in college, as more male students major in economics and the sciences and more female students in the arts, languages, and humanities. In the work force, more men become doctors, construction workers, auto mechanics, airplane pilots, investment bankers, and engineers. In contrast, more women become secretaries, schoolteachers, nurses, flight attendants, bank tellers, and housewives.

Back on the home front, the life cycle begins again when a man and woman have their first baby and discover that "It's a girl!" or "It's a boy!" The traditional pinks and blues are not as distinct as they used to be. Many gender barriers of the past have been broken down, and the colors have somewhat blended together. Nevertheless, **sexism**—prejudice and discrimination based on a person's gender—still exists. Indeed, it begins with the fact that sex is the most conspicuous social category we use to identify ourselves and others.

Exercise 4 **Discussion and Critical Thinking**

1. What are the subject and focus parts of the topic sentence? Hint: The topic sentence is toward the end of the paragraph.

2. Is Brehm trying mainly to inform, to persuade, or both? Explain.

3. Is this paragraph more comparison or contrast? Give evidence.

4. What points does Brehm use?

5. Does Brehm use the alternating or opposing pattern?

6. Given a choice, would girls naturally choose dolls and boys trucks? In other words, are boys and girls just genetically different in that respect? Discuss.

7. Does your experience tell you that Brehm is right or wrong? If she is right, would you use the terms "prejudice and discrimination" to characterize the situation? If she is correct, how would one explain the statistical fact that, overall, for the current generation, females are better educated than men?

Topics for Paragraphs of Comparison and Contrast

Most of these topics can also be used for short essays.

Reading-Based Writing Topics

See Chapter 3 for instruction and examples for writing summaries, reactions, and two-part responses (separate paragraphs of summary and reaction). Use quotations and references. Credit source(s).

"Two Loves: Puppy and True"

1. Using the terms from this paragraph, write a comparison-and-contrast paragraph on a puppy-love couple and a true-love couple you know. Your subject could be one couple at different stages of their relationship.

"A Summary of 'The Messy Are in Denial'"

2. Use ideas about orderly and disorderly people found in Walker's summary to write a comparison-and-contrast paragraph about a neat person and a messy person you know. Refer to and quote from Walker's summary.

"Blue as in *Boy*, Pink as in *Girl*"

3. Write a paragraph patterned on three or more of the main points of this reading selection—colors, names, toys, activities, college majors, careers—in which you discuss your own family or another family you know well, with attention to at least one male child and one female child. Be sure to use references to and quotations from this source.

General Topic

4. The following topics refer to general subjects. Provide specific names and other detailed information as you develop your ideas by using the 4 *P*'s (purpose, points, patterns, and presentation).

   a. Two automobiles
   b. Two fast-food restaurants
   c. Two homes
   d. Two people who play the same sport
   e. Two generations
   f. Two motorcycles, cars, or snowmobiles
   g. Two actors, singers, or musicians
   h. Two ways of learning
   i. Two ways of controlling
   j. Two kinds of child care
   k. Two mothers: one who stays at home and one who works outside the home

Cross-Curricular Topics

5. In the fields of nutritional science and health, compare and contrast two diets, two exercise programs, or two pieces of exercise equipment.
6. Compare and contrast your field of study (or one aspect of it) as it existed some time ago (specify the years) and as it is now. Refer to new developments and discoveries, such as scientific breakthroughs and technological advances.

Career-Related Topics

7. Compare and contrast two products or services, with the purpose of showing that one is better.
8. Compare and contrast two management styles or two work styles.
9. Compare and contrast two career fields to show that one is better for you.
10. Compare and contrast a public school and a business.
11. Compare and contrast an athletic team and a business.

Writer's Guidelines at a Glance:
Comparison and Contrast

1. Work with the 4 *P*'s:

   ▪ **Purpose:** Decide whether you want to
     inform (show relationships) or to persuade (show that one side
     is better).
   ▪ **Points:** Decide which ideas you will apply to each side. Consider
     beginning by making a list from which to select.
   ▪ **Patterns:** Decide whether to use subject-by-subject or point-
     by-point organization.
   ▪ **Presentation:** Decide to what extent you should develop your
     ideas. Be sure to use cross-references to make connections and
     to use examples and details to support your views.

2. Your basic subject-by-subject outline will probably look like this:

   I. Subject 1
      A. Point 1
      B. Point 2
   II. Subject 2
      A. Point 1
      B. Point 2

3. Your basic point-by-point outline will probably look like this:

   I. Point 1
      A. Subject 1
      B. Subject 2
   II. Point 2
      A. Subject 1
      B. Subject 2

4. Use CLUESS for revision and COPS for editing. See pages 21–24
   for guidance.

12

Definition:
Clarifying Terms

∿ Writing Paragraphs of Definition

Most definitions are short; they consist of a **synonym** (a word that has the same meaning as the term to be defined), a phrase, or a sentence. For example, we might say that a hypocrite is a person "professing beliefs or virtues he or she does not possess." Terms can also be defined by **etymology**, or word history. *Hypocrite* once meant "actor" (*hypocrites*) in Greek because an actor was pretending to be someone else. We may find this information interesting and revealing, but the history of a word may be of limited use because the meaning has changed drastically over the years. Sometimes definitions occupy a paragraph or an entire essay. The short definition is called a **simple definition**; the longer one is known as an **extended definition**.

Techniques for Development

Paragraphs of definition can take many forms. Among the more common techniques for writing a paragraph of definition are the patterns we have worked with in previous chapters. Consider each of those patterns when you need to write an extended definition. For a particular term, some forms will be more useful than others; use the pattern that best fulfills your purpose.

Each of the following questions takes a pattern of writing and directs it toward definition.

- **Narration:** Can I tell an anecdote or a story to define this subject (such as *jerk*, *humanitarian*, or *patriot*)? This form may overlap with description and exemplification.
- **Description:** Can I describe this subject (such as *a whale* or *the moon*)?

- **Exemplification:** Can I give examples of this subject (such as naming individuals to provide examples of *actors, diplomats,* or *satirists*)?
- **Analysis by division:** Can I divide this subject into parts (for example, the parts of *a heart, a cell,* or *a carburetor*)?
- **Process analysis:** Can I define this subject (such as *lasagna, a tornado, a hurricane, blood pressure,* or any number of scientific processes) by describing how to make it or how it occurs? Common to the methodology of communicating in science, this approach is sometimes called the "operational definition."
- **Cause and effect:** Can I define this subject (such as *a flood, a drought, a riot,* or *a cancer*) by its causes and effects?
- **Classification:** Can I group this subject (such as kinds of *families, cultures, religions,* or *governments*) into classes?

Subject	Class	Characteristics
A republic	is a form of government	in which power resides in the people (the electorate).

- **Comparison and contrast:** Can I define this subject (such as *extremist* or *patriot*) by explaining what it is similar to and different from? If you are defining *orangutan* for a person who has never heard of one but has heard of the gorilla, then you could make comparison-and-contrast statements. If you want to define *patriot,* you might want to stress what it is not (the contrast) before you explain what it is: a patriot is not a one-dimensional flag waver, not someone who hates "foreigners" because America is always right and always best.

When you develop ideas for a definition paragraph, use a cluster to consider all the paragraph patterns you have learned. Put a double bubble around the subject to be defined. Then put a single bubble around the paragraph patterns and add appropriate words. If a paragraph pattern is not relevant to what you are defining, leave it blank. If you want to expand your range of information, you could add a bubble for a simple dictionary definition and another for an etymological definition. The bubble cluster on page 151 shows how a term could be defined using different paragraph patterns.

Order

The organization of your extended definition is likely to be one of emphasis, but it may be space or time, depending on the subject material. You may use just one pattern of development for the overall sequence. Use the principles of organization discussed in previous chapters.

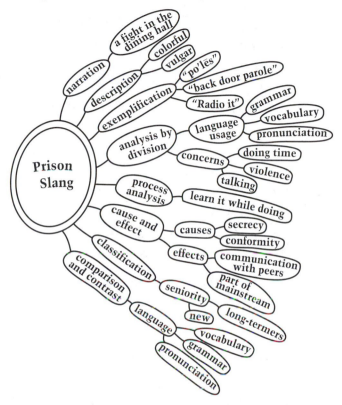

Introduction and Development

Consider these ways of introducing a definition: with a question, with a statement of what the subject is not, with a statement of what the word or phrase originally meant, or with a discussion of why a clear definition is important. You may use a combination of these ways or all of them before you continue with your definition.

Development, whether in the form of sentences for the paragraph or of paragraphs for the essay, is likely to represent one or more of the patterns of narration, description, exposition (with its own subdivisions), and argumentation.

Whether you personalize a definition depends on your purpose and your audience. Your instructor may ask you to write about a word within the context of your experience or to write about it from a detached, clinical viewpoint.

Transitional Words

Consider using the following transitional words to improve coherence by connecting ideas with ideas, sentences with sentences, and paragraphs with paragraphs:

*   **FOR DEFINITION:** *originates from, means, derives from, refers to, for example, as a term, as a concept, label, similar to, different from, in a particular context, in common usage, in historical context*

∼ Practicing Patterns of Definition

Exercise 1 Completing Patterns

Fill in the following double bubble with a term to be defined. You might want to define culturally diverse society, educated person, leader, role model, friend, puppy love, true love, success, *or intelligence. Then fill in at least one more bubble on the right for each paragraph pattern. If the pattern does not apply (that is, if it would not provide useful information for your definition), mark it NA ("not applicable").*

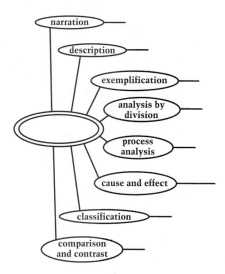

～ Examining Patterns of Definition

Student Writing

Going Too Far

Linda Wong

After hearing people say, "I just can't love him [or her] enough" and also "It was too much of a good thing," Linda Wong set out to explore the definition of the word extremist.

<table>
<tr>
<td>What the term does not mean</td>
<td>Some people believe that it is good to be an extremist in some areas, but those people are actually changing the meaning of the</td>
</tr>
<tr>
<td>Simple definition</td>
<td>word. According to the Random House Dictionary of the English Language, the word <u>extremism</u> itself means "excessively biased</td>
</tr>
<tr>
<td>Topic sentence</td>
<td>ideas, intemperate conduct." <u>The extremist goes too far; that means going too far in whatever the person is doing.</u> I once heard someone say that it is good for people to be extremists in love. But that is not true. <u>It</u></td>
</tr>
<tr>
<td>Example/ contrast</td>
<td><u>is good to be enthusiastically and sincerely in love, but extremists in love love excessively and intemperately.</u> People who love well may be tender and sensitive and attentive, but extremists are possessive or smothering. The same can be said of parents.</td>
</tr>
<tr>
<td>Example/ contrast</td>
<td><u>We all want to be good parents, but parental extremists involve themselves too much in the lives of their children,</u> who, in turn, may find it difficult to develop as individuals and become independent. Even in patriotism, good patriots are to be distinguished from</td>
</tr>
<tr>
<td>Example/ contrast</td>
<td>extreme patriots. <u>Good patriots love their country, but extreme patriots love their country so much that they think citizens from other countries are inferior and suspect.</u></td>
</tr>
</table>

	Extreme patriots may have Hitler-like

Extreme patriots may have Hitler-like
tendencies. Just what is wrong with
extremists then? It is the loss of

Examples   perspective. <u>The extremists are so
preoccupied with one concern that they lose
their sense of balance.</u> They are the
<u>workaholics</u>, the <u>zealots</u>, the <u>superpatriots</u>
of the world. They may begin with a good
objective, but they focus on it so much that
they can become destructive, obnoxious, and

Effect and   often pitiful. <u>The worst effect is that these</u>
concluding   <u>extremists lose their completeness as human</u>
sentence   <u>beings.</u>

▋Exercise 2▐ Discussion and Critical Thinking

1. Wong says that extremists "can become destructive, obnoxious, and often pitiful." Can you think of any good effects from people who are extremists? For example, what about a scientist who works fifteen hours a day to find a cure for a horrible disease? Is it possible that the scientist may succeed in his or her profession and fail in his or her personal life? But what if the scientist does not want a personal life? Discuss.

2. Why does Wong use contrast so much?

3. According to Wong, would it be bad for a person to be an extremist in religion? Discuss.

Prison Slang

Ruby Red

Because prison is a unique community with edgy and tenuous relationships, it is predictable that it would have its own variety of language. For student Ruby Red (pseudonym), knowing prison slang is crucial to her well-being.

Topic sentence and basic definition	Prison slang is like other slang in that it is language that is used in a special way for special reasons. Like conventional slang,
Comparison	some words have unusual, nonstandard meanings, and some words are invented. Most slang is used by people who want to conform to group language customs. In prison it is used both by people who don't want others to know what they are talking about and by those who are seeking group identity. As a variety
More basic definition	of language, it is like a dialect because it is just part of the culture of that group.
Classification (areas)	Prison slang covers many areas, but it especially reflects prisoners' concerns: violence, talking, and reputation. The very
Examples follow	idea of violence is strangely muted by the terms used to discuss brutal acts. If a person is attacked by a group of people who throw a blanket over her head before they beat her, she is said to be the recipient of a "blanket party" given by a "rat pack." If she "caught a cold" or they "took her wind," she died. They may have killed her with a sharp instrument called a "shank" or a "shiv." Perhaps she didn't know there was a "raven" (contract) out on her; she thought they were only "putting on a floor show" (pretending) or "selling wolf tickets" (bluffing). She should have listened to their talk more carefully. They said she had

"snitched them off" (informed), and her friend had "pulled her coat" (told her something she should know), but then a cop came by and she said, "Radio it, dog-face it, dummy up" (all meaning "shut up"), and then she "put it on hold" (filed it away for future use). That was her mistake because the woman out to get her was a "die hard, hard core, cold piece" (each meaning "career criminal"), who was a "hog" (enforcer), "dancer" (fighter), and a "jive bitch"

Concluding statement (agitator). <u>These are only a few of the hundreds of slang words used by women behind bars. They are an important part of prison life.</u>

Exercise 3 Discussion and Critical Thinking

1. The paragraph begins with a topic sentence and a basic definition. What form (topic sentence and support, or topic sentence, support, and concluding sentence) does it take?

2. How is prison slang actually an integral part of the culture?

3. With what is prison slang compared? Is that a valid and useful comparison? Discuss.

4. What is the main pattern (narration, description, exemplification, analysis by division, cause and effect) used in explaining prison slang?

5. What other patterns are used?

6. How are examples grouped, or classified?

7. After reading this paragraph carefully, do you think of prison as a place of constant tension and violence or as a complex society with many concerns?

Professional Writing

Burnout
Gregory Moorhead and Ricky W. Griffin

> *Occupational sociologists Gregory Moorhead and Ricky W. Griffin provide the following definition of burnout adapted from their book* Organizational Behavior *(2001). Their definition pertains mainly to vocational work, but burnout can occur in any organization— church, government, recreation, even marriage and family.*

Burnout, a consequence of stress, has clear implications for both people and organizations. Burnout is a general feeling of exhaustion that develops when a person simultaneously experiences too much pressure and has too few sources of satisfaction. Burnout usually develops in the following way. First, people with high aspirations and strong motivation to get things done are prime candidates for burnout under certain conditions. They are especially vulnerable when the organization suppresses or limits their initiative while constantly demanding that they serve the organization's own ends. In such a situation, the individual is likely to put too much of himself or herself into the job. In other words, the person may well keep trying to meet his or her own agenda while simultaneously trying to fulfill the organization's expectations. The most likely effects of this situation are prolonged stress, fatigue, frustration, and helplessness under the burden of overwhelming demands. The person literally exhausts his or her aspiration and motivation, much as a candle burns itself out. Loss of self-confidence and psychological withdrawal follow. Ultimately, burnout results. At this point, the individual may start dreading going to work in the morning, may put in longer hours but accomplish less than before, and may generally display mental and physical exhaustion.

Exercise 4 Discussion and Critical Thinking

1. Does the first sentence or the second sentence provide a better definition? Which one is the topic sentence for the paragraph? What are the subject and the focus parts of the topic sentence?

2. What other pattern—comparison and contrast, classification, cause and effect, or narration—provides structure for this definition? Explain.

3. If you were going to personalize this definition, what other pattern(s) would you use? Explain.

〜 Topics for Paragraphs of Definition

Most of these topics can also be used for short essays.

Reading-Based Writing Topics

See Chapter 3 for instruction and examples for writing summaries, reactions, and two-part responses (separate paragraphs of summary and reaction). Use quotations and references. Credit source(s).

"Going Too Far"

1. Apply the definition of *extremist* from Linda Wong's paragraph to a situation you are familiar with: an overprotective parent, a controlling companion, an overly controlling boss, a too strict police officer or teacher, a too virtuous friend, a preacher, a too-clean housekeeper (companion, parent), a zealous patriot, a person fanatical about a diet, a person concerned too much with good health or exercise. You might begin your paragraph with the statement: "Nothing is good when carried to the extreme." Or "It is good to be _____, but when _____ is carried to the extreme, the result is _____."

"Burnout"

2. Borrow the definition from this paragraph (but give credit) and develop it with an extended example of someone you know who is or was a burnout. The definition is likely to be developed as a narrative around a set of causes and effects. Think of those who may be temporarily or terminally burned out—those drained of enthusiasm, feeling, and direction and those reduced to shambling, hollow-eyed hulks: bosses, workers, teachers and students, parents and offspring, young and old. Perhaps you would like to write about a person who seemed clinically burned out but then experienced a rekindling of flames (if so, who or what lit the fire)? Use references and quotations.

General Topics

3. Write a definition of "_____ slang." That variety of slang comes from a generation (your generation, especially of your social group), a blend of English and another language (such as Spanish and English—Spanglish; Chinese and English—Chineselish), a gang, a work-centered group (jargon), or a men's

prison. Use numerous examples. Consider organizing your definition around various situations in which the slang would be used. For a useful model definition on a similar subject, review "Prison Slang" on page 155.

4. Write an extended definition about one of the following terms:

    a. Workaholic
    b. Sexist
    c. Liberated woman
    d. Sexual harassment
    e. Macho
    f. Soul food, ethnic food (any one), fast food, McFood
    g. Rap music, or specific form
    h. Form of music, such as rockabilly, hip-hop, rap, techno, punk,
    i. Street smart, school smart, sports smart, work smart, party smart

Cross-Curricular Topics

5. Define one of the following terms in a paragraph:

    a. History and government: socialism, democracy, patriotism, capitalism, communism
    b. Philosophy: existentialism, free will, determinism, ethics, stoicism
    c. Education: charter schools, school choice, gifted program, ESL (English as a second language), paired teaching, digital school
    d. Music: symphony, sonata, orchestra, tonic systems
    e. Health science: autism, circulatory system, respiratory system, thyroid, cancer, herbal remedies, acupuncture
    f. Marketing: depression, digitalization, discretionary income, electronic commerce, globalization, marketing channel, free trade, telemarketing, warehouse clubs

Career-Related Topic

6. Define one of the following terms by using the appropriate pattern(s) of development (such as exemplification, cause and effect, narration, comparison and contrast, description, analysis by division, and process analysis: *total quality management, quality control, downsizing, outsourcing, business ethics, customer satisfaction, cost effectiveness.*

Writer's Guidelines at a Glance: Definition

1. Use clustering to consider other patterns of development that may be used to define your term.

2. The organization of your extended definition is likely to be one of emphasis, but it may be space or time, depending on the subject. You may use just one pattern of development for the overall organization.

3. Consider these ways of introducing a definition: with a question, with a statement of what the subject is not, with a statement of what the word or phrase originally meant, or with a discussion of why a clear definition is important. You may use a combination of these ways before you continue with your definition.

4. Whether you personalize a definition depends on your purpose and your audience. Your instructor may ask you to write about a word within the context of your own experience or to write about it from a detached, clinical viewpoint.

5. Use CLUESS for revision and COPS for editing. See pages 21–24 for guidance.

13

Argument:
Writing to Influence

~ Writing Paragraphs of Argument

Persuasion and Argument Defined

Persuasion is a broad term; when we persuade, we try to influence people to think in a certain way or to do something. **Argument** is persuasion on a topic about which reasonable people disagree. Argument involves controversy. Whereas exercising appropriately is probably not controversial because reasonable people do not dispute the idea, an issue such as gun control is controversial. In this chapter, we will be concerned mainly with the kind of persuasion that involves argument.

Components of Your Paragraph

Statements of argument are informal or formal in design. Although an opinion column in a newspaper is likely to have little set structure, an argument in college writing is likely to be tightly organized. Nevertheless, the opinion column and the college paper have much in common. Both provide a proposition, which is the main point of the argument, and both provide support, which is the evidence or the reasons that back up the proposition.

For a well-structured paragraph, an organizational plan is desirable. Consider these elements—background, proposition, qualification of proposition, refutation, and support—when you write a paragraph of argument, and ask yourself the following questions as you develop your ideas:

- **Background:** What is the historical or social context for this controversial issue?
- **Proposition** (the **topic sentence** of a paragraph of argument): What do I want my audience to believe or to do?

162

- **Qualification of proposition:** Can I limit my proposition so that those who disagree cannot easily challenge me with exceptions? If, for example, I am in favor of using animals for scientific experimentation, am I concerned only with medical experiments or with any use, including that pertaining to the cosmetic industry?
- **Refutation** (taking the opposing view into account, mainly to point out its fundamental weakness): What is the view on the other side, and why is it flawed in reasoning or evidence?
- **Support:** In addition to sound reasoning, can I use appropriate facts, examples, statistics, and opinions of authorities?

The basic form for a paragraph of argument includes the proposition (the topic sentence) and support. The support sentences are, in effect, *because* statements; that is, the proposition is valid *because* of the support. Your organization should look something like this:

> *Proposition (topic sentence):* It is time to pass a national law restricting smoking in public places.
>
> I. Discomfort of the nonsmoker (support 1)
> II. Health of the nonsmoker (support 2)
> III. Cost to the nation (support 3)

Kinds of Evidence

In addition to sound reasoning, you can use the following kinds of evidence, or support.

1. **Facts.** Martin Luther King Jr. was killed in Memphis, Tennessee, on April 4, 1968. Because an event that has happened is true and can be verified, this statement about King is a fact. But that James Earl Ray acted alone in killing King is to some a questionable fact. That King was the greatest of all civil rights leaders is also opinion because it cannot be verified.

   Some facts are readily accepted because they are general knowledge—you and your reader know them to be true because they can be or have been verified. Other "facts" are based on personal observation and are reported in various publications but may be false or questionable. You should always be concerned about the reliability of the source for both the information you use and the information used by those with other viewpoints. Still other so-called facts are genuinely debatable because of their complexity or the incompleteness of the knowledge available.

2. **Examples.** You must present a sufficient number of examples, and the examples must be relevant.

3. **Statistics.** Statistics are facts and data of a numerical kind that are classified and tabulated to present significant information about a given subject.

Avoid presenting a long list of figures; select statistics carefully and relate them to things familiar to your reader. The millions of dollars spent on a war in a single week, for example, become more comprehensible when expressed in terms of what the money would purchase in education, highways, or urban renewal.

To test the validity of statistics, either yours or your opponent's, ask: Who gathered them? Under what conditions? For what purpose? How are they used?

4. **Evidence from, and opinions of, authorities.** Most readers accept facts from recognized, reliable sources—government publications, standard reference works, and books and periodicals published by established firms. In addition, readers will accept evidence and opinions from individuals who, because of their knowledge and experience, are recognized as experts.

In using authoritative sources as proof, keep these points in mind:

- Select authorities who are generally recognized as experts in their field.
- Use authorities who qualify in the field pertinent to your argument.
- Select authorities whose views are not biased.
- Try to use several authorities.
- Identify an authority's credentials clearly in your paragraph.

Transitional Words

Consider using the following transitional words to improve coherence by connecting ideas with ideas, sentences with sentences, and paragraphs with paragraphs:

- **FOR ARGUMENT:** *it follows that, as a result, causes taken collectively, as a concession, even though, of course, in the context of, in the light of, in the final analysis, following this, further, as additional support, moreover, consequently, according to, in support of, contrary to, therefore, naturally*

∿ Practicing Patterns of Argument

Exercise 1 Completing Patterns

Fill in the blanks in the following outlines with supporting state-
ments for each proposition. Each outline uses this pattern:

> Proposition
>   I. Support
>   II. Support
>   III. Support

1. Proposition: College athletes should be paid.

    I. _____

    II. They work long hours in practice and competition.

    III. They have less time than many other students for study.

2. Proposition: Zoos are beneficial institutions.

    I. _____

    II. They preserve endangered species by captive breeding.

    III. They study animal diseases and find cures.

∿ Examining Paragraphs of Argument

Student Writing

My Life to Live—or Not

Angela DeSarro

After Angela DeSarro received a list of topics from which to select,
she went to the library to obtain some information about the ones
that interested her. One such topic was euthanasia. Her electronic
data bank offered her an essay in the Journal of the American
Medical Association *about a doctor who illegally assisted a suf-*
fering, terminally ill patient. DeSarro's mind and emotions came
together on the issue and she had her topic.

```
          Debbie, 20, was dying of ovarian cancer.
     Racked with pain, nauseous, emaciated, she
     sought the ultimate relief and found it in
     euthanasia. A doctor administered a drug and
```

she died. It was a hidden, secret act. It was
also illegal in Debbie's state, but this case
was written up in the *Journal of the American
Medical Association.* <u>Surely the time has come</u>
Proposition   <u>for a nationwide law legalizing this practice</u>
<u>under specific provisions and regulations.</u>
Debbie had reached the point of not only
<u>enduring terrible pain</u> but of <u>vomiting</u>
<u>constantly</u> and <u>not being able to sleep.</u> <u>Pain-</u>
Support   <u>killing medication no longer worked.</u> She
wanted to die with what she regarded as a
degree of dignity. She had already become a
withered, suffering human being with tubes
coming out of her nose, throat, and urinary
tract, and she was losing all self-control.
Support   <u>She also believed that it should be up to</u>
<u>her, under these conditions, to decide when</u>
<u>and how she should die.</u> Laws in most places
prohibit terminally ill patients from
choosing death and physicians from assisting
them. One state, Oregon, has a law favoring
physician-assisted suicide, at least in the
limited cases of terminally ill people
expected to live less than six months.
Concluding   Numerous people have benefited from that law;
sentence as a   it was not abused. <u>It, or a similar form,</u>
restated   <u>should be enacted nationwide.</u>
proposition

Exercise 2 Discussion and Critical Thinking

1. What kinds of evidence (facts, example(s), statement by expert)
   does DeSarro use to support her argument?

2. What might be the objections to her reasoned argument?

3. Do you agree or disagree with DeSarro's argument? Why?

Summary of "Bully, Bully" by John Leo
Susan Aragon

Susan Aragon's assignment was to write a summary of an essay in her college English textbook. The summary required her to be brief, to concentrate on the main ideas, to use few quotations, and to be objective.

In writing "Bully, Bully," John Leo is concerned mainly with the definition of *bullying*. He is opposed to bullying as he defines it: the physical kind. He says parents and schools should do whatever is necessary to identify and stop it. They should protect those being bullied; punish the offenders; and help both those being bullied and the bullies, who are often bullied themselves. But he disagrees with those who have what he calls an "elastic" definition, one that covers "verbal (e.g., name calling, threats), physical (e.g., hitting), or psychological (e.g., shunning/exclusion)" behaviors. To the contrary, he believes that "hard looks," "stare-downs," "spreading rumors," "dirty looks," "teasing," "shunning," and "exclusion" are ordinary experiences of growing up.

Children will do those things, he says, and to
include those behaviors in a definition of
bullying will mean that almost everyone is a
bully. He believes that this movement is an
attempt to overregulate the young, and that the
whole thing is part of a worldwide campaign by
some groups and individuals to regulate
behavior, such as sexual harassment, in the
adult world and the workplace as well. He says,
"It's time to stop and ask: Where is our
antibullying campaign going?"

Work Cited

Leo, John. "Bully, Bully." *Paragraphs and
Essays: With Integrated Readings.* Ed.
Lee Brandon and Kelly Brandon. 11th ed.
Boston: Cengage, 2011. 320-22. Print.

Exercise 3 Discussion and Critical Thinking

1. What does Leo mean by "elastic definition"? Does this
approximate the definition you are familiar with or is it broader
and more detailed? Explain.

2. What are the three parts of the definition Leo questions?

3. What part(s) of the definition does he disagree with and why does
he hold his view?

4. Explain why you agree or disagree with Leo.

5. The injuries caused by physical assaults are easily identified.
   What about the injuries caused by psychological assaults?
   Are they to be largely discounted and seen as part of growing up,
   or are they to be seen as a significant part of bullying and
   something that need be corrected?

Professional Writing

A Modest Proposal: Guys Shouldn't Drive Till 25
Joyce Gallagher

> *Freelance writer Joyce Gallagher says we should look at the
> national problem of motor vehicle accidents and apply the
> brakes. To Gallagher, statistics tell the story, and the solution is
> as inevitable to her as it may be unthinkable to you.*

In the year 2001, 57,480 people were killed in motor vehicle
accidents.* That figure is within a few hundred of being the same
number as those killed in the Vietnam War. We took drastic
measures back in the early 1970s and ended that war in a way
shocking to some: we left. The time has come for another drastic
scheme. We need to recognize the main causes of this highway
carnage and take action. According to the U.S. Department of
Transportation, 25.1 percent of the roadway fatalities involve an
age group constituting only 14.5 percent of the driving public.
That group is the age range from 15 to 25. Within that group, one
half are males. They are three times more likely to be involved in
roadway fatalities, meaning that about 7 percent of the males are
responsible for more than 16 percent of roadway fatalities. This

---

*All statistics in this article are from the U.S. Bureau of Transportation Statistics:
www.bts.gov.

proposal may be a hard sell for politicians, but it is time for us to step forward boldly and raise the legal driving age for males nationally to 25, with exceptions only for those in the military and those in emergency positions, such as fire fighting and law enforcement. Some may protest that it is unfair to punish the good young male drivers for the sins of their irresponsible peers. But we're already discriminating by group. Surely we all agree that drivers under a certain age should not be allowed to drive. That age varies from state to state, but it is around 15. We have concluded that those younger than 15 are too immature. We don't say those under 15 should be treated individually, not even on the basis of gender. Instead, we exclude the offending group. With my proposal, we would simply move the legal age of male drivers to 25, lumping those of similar age and same gender together for the good of society. Some might argue that improved drivers' education programs in our school system, better public transportation, the production of vehicles that are no more powerful and threatening than they need be, a reduced speed limit, counseling and restrictions for repeat offenders, and a stricter enforcement of existing laws represent a wiser approach to our national problem. However, because those ideas have failed to resonate, and young males have continued to put the pedal to the metal in a flood of blood, it is time for a simple statement that will fit on your bumper sticker:

Guys Shouldn't Drive Till 25

▮Exercise 4▮ Discussion and Critical Thinking

1. Underline the proposition, and underline and label the subject and focus parts.

2. How is the proposition introduced (history, testimony, statistics, question) in the first paragraph?

3. How does Gallagher qualify (limit) her proposition? Copy the
   last part of the sentence that states the qualifications.

4. Would this law create some problems not discussed by the
   author? If so, what kind?

5. Which parts of the argument would you disagree with
   and why?

6. Do you think the author is entirely serious about this argument?
   What author comments might suggest that she is not?

7. Does it make any difference that the author is female?
   Why or why not?

〰 Topics for Paragraphs of Argument

Most of these topics can also be used for short essays.

Reading-Based Writing Topics

See Chapter 3 for instruction and examples for writing summaries, reactions, and two-part responses (separate paragraphs of summary and reaction). Use quotations and references. Credit source(s).

"My Life to Live—or Not"

1. Write an argument in which you agree or disagree with DeSarro. Incorporate your own value system, religious or secular, into your discussion. Use references and quotations.
2. Use the Internet or the library to research the state law in Oregon that permits doctors to assist in suicides under certain conditions. Discuss how well the law has worked and whether it should be enacted as a national law or a law in other states.

"Summary of 'Bully, Bully' by John Leo"

3. Write a reaction to the ideas in this summary. Evaluate Leo's views on the overregulation of young people. To what extent do you agree with him? Do you agree that "'hard looks,' 'stare-downs' 'spreading rumors,' 'dirty looks,' 'teasing,' 'shunning,' and 'exclusion' are ordinary experiences of growing up,' and comparatively not so damaging? Consider what you know about bullying of all forms and interpretations in K-12, including cyberbullying. Use references to and quotations from the summary.

"A Modest Proposal: Guys Shouldn't Drive Till 25"

4. Write an argument in which you either agree or disagree with Gallagher's views. Refer to and quote from the paragraph. Make it a critique of specifically what she said and what you think she means. Consider using examples from your own experience and observations.
5. Write a paragraph or an essay in which you discuss Gallagher's purpose and technique. Is Gallagher serious in what she is saying, or does she exaggerate to make her point? What phrases or ideas suggest her tone? Be specific and document your work. The title is based on a famous work by Jonathan Swift: "A Modest Proposal." You can find a copy on the Internet by keying in

"Jonathan Swift" and "A Modest Proposal" on a search engine such as Google. Explain how being familiar with Swift's essay helps you understand Gallagher's message.

General Topic

6. Write a paragraph on one of the following broad subject areas. You will have to limit your focus for a paragraph of argument. You may also modify the topics to fit specific situations.

   a. Banning pit bulls
   b. School dress codes
   c. Sex education
   d. Sexual harassment
   e. Advertising tobacco
   f. Zone changes for stores selling liquor
   g. Curfew for teenagers
   h. Laws keeping known gang members out of parks

Cross-Curricular Topic

7. From a class you are taking or have taken, or from your major area of study, select an issue on which thoughtful people may disagree, and write a paragraph of persuasion or argument. It could be an interpretation of an ambiguous piece of literature for an English class; a position on global warming, public land management, or the Endangered Species Act for a class in ecology; a paper arguing about the effectiveness of government regulation in a political-science class; a view on a certain kind of diet in a food-science class; a preference for a particular worldview in a class on philosophy; or an assertion on the proper role of chiropractors as health-care practitioners in a health-science class.

Career-Related Topic

8. Write a persuasive paragraph in which you argue to solve a problem pertaining to one of the following workplace issues:

   a. Labor unions: strikes, recruiting, open shop, closed shop, right-to-work states
   b. Doing your job (or part of it) at home rather than at the workplace
   c. Fringe benefits: health care, vacations, severance pay

    d. Evaluation procedures
    e. Staggering lunch hours and work breaks
    f. Outsourcing jobs

Writer's Guidelines at a Glance: Argument

1. Consider which aspects of the formal argument you need for your paragraph:

   - **Background:** What is the historical or social context for this controversial issue?
   - **Proposition** (the **topic sentence**): What do I want my audience to believe or to do?
   - **Qualification of proposition:** Have I limited my proposition so that those who disagree with me cannot easily challenge me with exceptions?
   - **Refutation** (taking the opposing view into account, mainly to point out its fundamental weakness): What is the view on the other side, and why is it flawed in reasoning or evidence?
   - **Support:** In addition to sound reasoning, have I used appropriate facts, examples, statistics, and opinions of authorities?

2. The basic pattern of a paragraph of argument is likely to be in this form:

       Proposition (the topic sentence)
          I. Support 1
         II. Support 2
        III. Support 3

3. Use CLUESS for revision and COPS for editing. See pages 21–24 for guidance.

14

Handbook

This chapter presents rules and examples for grammar, usage, punctuation, capitalization, spelling, and ESL matters.

〜 Identifying Parts of Speech

To classify a word as a part of speech, we observe two simple principles:

- The word must be in the context of communication, usually in a sentence.
- We must be able to identify the word with others that have similar characteristics—the eight parts of speech: nouns, pronouns, verbs, adjectives, adverbs, prepositions, conjunctions, or interjections.

The first principle is important because some words can be any of several parts of speech. The word *round*, for example, can function as five:

- I watched the potter *round* the block of clay. (verb)
- I saw her go *round* the corner. (preposition)
- She has a *round* head. (adjective)
- The astronauts watched the world go *round*. (adverb)
- The champ knocked him out in one *round*. (noun)

1. Nouns

a. **Nouns are naming words.** Nouns may name persons, animals, plants, places, things, substances, qualities, or ideas—for example, *Bart, armadillo, Mayberry, tree, rock, cloud, love, ghost, music, virtue.*

b. **Nouns are often pointed out by noun indicators.** These noun indicators—*the, a, an*—signal that a noun is ahead, although there may be words between the indicator and the noun itself.

the slime	*a* werewolf	*an* aardvark
the green slime	*a* hungry werewolf	*an* angry aardvark

2. Pronouns

A **pronoun** is a word that is used in place of a noun.

a. Some pronouns may represent specific persons or things:

I	she	they	you
me	her	them	yourself
myself	herself	themselves	yourselves
it	he	we	who
itself	him	us	whom
that	himself	ourselves	

b. Indefinite pronouns refer to nouns (persons, places, things) in a general way:

    each   everyone   nobody   somebody

c. Other pronouns point out particular things:

SINGULAR *this, that*   PLURAL *these, those*
           This is my treasure.   *These* are my jewels.
           That is your junk.   *Those* are your trinkets.

d. Still other pronouns introduce questions.

    Which is the best DVD player?

    What are the main ingredients of a Twinkie?

3. Verbs

Verbs show action or express being in relation to the subject of a sentence. They customarily occur in set positions in sentences.

a. **Action verbs** are usually easy to identify.

    The aardvark *ate* the crisp, tasty ants. (action verb)

    The aardvark *washed* them down with a snoutful of water. (action verb)

b. The ***being*** **verbs** are few in number and are also easy to identify. The most common *being* verbs are *is, was, were, are,* and *am.*

Gilligan *is* on an island in the South Pacific. (*being* verb)

I *am* his enthusiastic fan. (*being* verb)

c. The form of a verb expresses its tense, that is, the time of the action or being. The time may be in the present or past.

Roseanne *sings* "The Star-Spangled Banner." (present)

Roseanne *sang* "The Star-Spangled Banner." (past)

d. One or more **helping verbs** may be used with the main verb to form other tenses. The combination is called a **verb phrase.**

She *had sung* the song many times in the shower. (Helping verb and main verb indicate a time in the past.)

She *will be singing* the song no more in San Diego. (Helping verbs and main verb indicate a time in the future.)

e. Some helping verbs can be used alone as main verbs: *has, have, had, is, was, were, are,* and *am.* Certain other helping verbs function only as helpers: *will, shall, should,* and *could.*

The most common position for the verb is directly after the subject or after the subject and its modifiers.

At high noon only two men [subject] *were* on Main Street.

The man with the faster draw [subject and modifiers] *walked* away alone.

4. Adjectives

Adjectives modify nouns and pronouns. Most adjectives answer the questions *What kind? Which one?* and *How many?*

a. Adjectives answering the *What kind?* question are descriptive. They tell the quality, kind, or condition of the nouns or pronouns they modify.

red convertible	*dirty* fork
noisy muffler	*wild* roses
The rain is *gentle.*	Bob was *tired.*

b. Adjectives answering the *Which one?* question narrow or restrict the meaning of a noun. Some of these are pronouns that become adjectives by function.

my money	*our* ideas	the *other* house
this reason	*these* apples	

c. Adjectives answering the *How many?* question are, of course, numbering words.

some people   *each* pet   *few* goals
three dollars   *one* glove

d. The words *a*, *an*, and *the* are adjectives called **articles**. As noun indicators, they point out persons, places, and things.

5. Adverbs

a. **Adverbs** modify verbs, adjectives, and other adverbs. Adverbs answer the questions *How? Where? When?* and *To what degree?*

MODIFYING VERBS   They <u>did</u> their work <u>quickly</u>.
                              v   adv

MODIFYING ADJECTIVES   They were <u>somewhat</u> <u>happy</u>.
                                  adv   adj

MODIFYING ADVERBS   He answered <u>very</u> <u>slowly</u>.
                                adv   adv

- Adverbs that answer the *How?* question are concerned with manner or way.

  She ate the snails *hungrily*.

  He snored *noisily*.

- Adverbs that answer the *Where?* question show location.

  They drove *downtown*.

  He stayed *behind*.

  She climbed *upstairs*.

- Adverbs that answer the *When?* question indicate time.

  The ship sailed *yesterday*.

  I expect an answer *soon*.

- Adverbs that answer the *To what degree?* question express extent.

  She is *entirely* correct.

  He was *somewhat* annoyed.

b. Most words ending in *-ly* are adverbs.

  He completed the task <u>skillfully</u>.
                         adv

She answered him <u>courteously</u>.
                       adv

However, there are a few exceptions.

The house provided a <u>lovely</u> view of the valley.
                                adj

Your goblin mask is <u>ugly</u>.
                          adj

6. Prepositions

a. A **preposition** is a word or group of words that function as a connective. The preposition connects its object(s) to some other? word(s) in the sentence. A preposition and its object(s)—usually a noun or pronoun—with modifiers make up a **prepositional phrase**.

Bart worked <u>against</u> great <u>odds</u>.
               prep   object
            prepositional phrase

Everyone <u>in his household</u> cheered his effort.
        prep   object
     prepositional phrase

Following are some of the most common prepositions:

about	before	but	into	past
above	behind	by	like	to
across	below	despite	near	toward
after	beneath	down	of	under
against	beside	for	off	until
among	between	from	on	upon
around	beyond	in	over	with

b. Some prepositions are composed of more than one word and are constructed using other parts of speech:

according to	as far as	because of	in spite of
ahead of	as well as	in back of	instead of
along with	aside from	in front of	together with

<u>According to</u> the weather <u>report</u>, a storm is forming.
     prep   object
        prepositional phrase

Caution: Do not confuse adverbs with prepositions.

I went *across* slowly. (without an object—adverb)
I went *across* the field. (with an object—preposition)
We walked *behind* silently. (without an object—adverb)
We walked *behind* the mall. (with an object—preposition)

7. Conjunctions

a. A **conjunction** connects and shows a relationship between words, phrases, or clauses. A **phrase** is two or more words acting as a part of speech. A **clause** is a group of words with a subject and a verb. An independent clause can stand by itself: *She plays bass guitar.* A dependent clause cannot stand by itself: *when she plays bass guitar.*

b. The two kinds of conjunctions are coordinating and subordinating.

- **Coordinating conjunctions** connect words, phrases, and clauses of equal rank: noun with noun, adjective with adjective, verb with verb, phrase with phrase, main clause with main clause, and subordinate clause with subordinate clause. The seven common coordinating conjunctions are *for, and, nor, but, or, yet,* and *so.* (They form the acronym FANBOYS.)

  TWO NOUNS: Bring a <u>pencil</u> <u>and</u> some <u>paper.</u>
                          noun conj   noun

  TWO PHRASES: Did she go <u>to the store</u> <u>or</u> <u>to the game?</u>
                            prep phrase conj   prep phrase

  Paired conjunctions such as *either/or, neither/nor,* or *both/and* are usually classed as coordinating conjunctions.

  <u>Neither</u> the coach <u>nor</u> the manager was at fault.
   conj   conj

- **Subordinating conjunctions** connect dependent clauses with main clauses. The most common subordinating conjunctions include the following:

after	because	provided	whenever
although	before	since	where
as	but that	so that	whereas
as if	if	till	wherever
as long as	in order that	until	
as soon as	notwithstanding	when	

If the dependent clause comes *before* the main clause, it is set off by a comma.

Although she was in pain, she stayed in the game.
conj   subj   verb

dependent clause

If the because comes *after* the main clause, it usually is *not* set off by a comma.

She stayed in the game *because* she was needed.
conj   subj   verb

dependent clause

Caution: Certain words can function as either conjunctions or prepositions. It is necessary to look ahead to see if the word introduces a clause with a subject and verb—conjunction function—or takes an object—preposition function. Some of the words with two functions are *after*, *for*, *since*, and *until*.

After the concert was over, we went home. (clause follows—conjunction)

After the concert, we went home. (object follows—preposition)

8. Interjections

a. An **interjection** conveys strong emotion or surprise. When an interjection appears alone, it is usually punctuated with an exclamation mark.

Wow!   Curses!   Cowabunga!   Yaba dabba do!

b. When an interjection appears as part of a sentence, it is usually followed by a comma.

Oh, I did not consider that problem.

c. The interjection may sound exciting, but it is seldom appropriate for college writing.

⌒ Locating Subjects and Verbs

The **subject** is what the sentence is about, and the **verb** indicates what the subject is doing or is being.

Subjects

You can recognize the **simple subject** by asking *Who?* or *What?* causes the action or expresses the state of being found in the verb.

1. The simple subject and the simple verb can be single or compound.

   My *friend* and *I* have much in common.

   My friend *came* and *left* a present.

2. Although the subject usually appears before the verb, it may follow the verb.

   From tiny acorns grow mighty *oaks.*

3. The **command**, or **imperative**, **sentence** has a "you" as the implied subject, and no stated subject.

   (You) Read the notes.

4. Be careful not to confuse a subject with an object of a preposition.

   The *foreman* [subject] of the *jury* [object of the preposition] directs discussion.

Verbs

Verbs show action or express being in relation to the subject of a sentence.

1. **Action verbs** show movement or accomplishment of an idea or a deed.

   He *dropped* the book. (movement)

   He *read* the book. (accomplishment)

2. ***Being*** verbs indicate existence.

   They *were* concerned.

3. Verbs may appear as single words or as phrases.

   He *led* the charge. (single word)

   She *is leading* the charge. (phrase)

4. Verbs that are joined by a coordinating conjunction such as *and* and *or* are called **compound verbs**.

   She *worked* for twenty-five years and *retired.*

5. Do not confuse verbs with **verbals**, verblike words that function as other parts of speech.

> The bird *singing* [participle acting as an adjective] in the tree is defending its territory.
>
> *Singing* [gerund acting as a noun subject] is fun.
>
> I want *to eat* [infinitive acting as a noun object].

6. Do not confuse **adverbs** such as *never, not,* and *hardly* with verbs; they only modify verbs.

7. Do not overlook a part of the verb that is separated from another in a question.

> Where *had* the defendant *gone* on that fateful night?

∼ Writing Different Kinds of Sentences

On the basis of number and kinds of clauses, sentences may be classified as simple, compound, complex, and compound-complex.

Clauses

1. A **clause** is a group of words with a subject and a verb that functions as a part or all of a complete sentence. There are two kinds of clauses: independent (main) and dependent (subordinate).

2. An **independent (main) clause** is a group of words with a subject and a verb that can stand alone and make sense. An independent clause expresses a complete thought by itself and can be written as a separate sentence.

> I have the money.

3. A **dependent clause** is a group of words with a subject and a verb that depends on a main clause to give it meaning. The dependent clause functions in the common sentence patterns as a noun, an adjective, or an adverb.

> When I have the money

Kinds of Sentences Defined

Kind	Definition	Example
1. Simple	One independent clause	She did the work well.
2. Compound	Two or more independent clauses (underlined)	She did the work well, and she was paid well.
3. Complex	One independent clause (underlined) and one or more dependent clauses (italicized)	*Because she did the work well*, she was paid well.
4. Compound-Complex	Two or more independent clauses and one or more dependent clauses	*Because she did the work well*, she was paid well, and she was satisfied.

Punctuation

1. Use a comma before a coordinating conjunction (*for, and, nor, but, or, yet, so*) between two independent clauses.

   The movie was good, *but* the tickets were expensive.

2. Use a comma after a dependent clause (beginning with a subordinating conjunction such as *because, although, when, since,* or *before*) that occurs before the main clause.

   When the bus arrived, we quickly boarded.

3. Use a semicolon between two independent clauses in one sentence if there is no coordinating conjunction.

   The bus arrived; we quickly boarded.

4. Use a semicolon before and usually a comma after a conjunctive adverb (such as *however, otherwise, therefore, on the other hand,* and *in fact*), and between two independent clauses (no comma after *then, also, now, thus,* and *soon*).

   The Dodgers have not played well this year; *however,* the Giants have won ten games in a row.

   Spring training went well; *then* the regular baseball season began.

〜 Combining Sentences

Coordination

If you intend to communicate two equally important and closely related ideas, you certainly will want to place them close together, probably in a **compound sentence** (two or more independent clauses).

1. When you combine two sentences by using a coordinating conjunction, drop the period, change the capital letter to a small letter, and insert a comma before the coordinating conjunction.

   He likes your home. He can visit for only three months.

   He likes your home, *but* he can visit for only three months.

2. When you combine two sentences by using a semicolon, replace the period with a semicolon and change the capital letter that begins the second sentence to a small letter. If you wish to use a conjunctive adverb, insert it after the semicolon and usually put a comma after it.

   He likes your home; he can visit for only three months.

   He likes your home; *however*, he can visit for only three months.

Subordination

If you have two ideas that are closely related but one is secondary to or dependent on the other, you may want to use a complex sentence.

   My neighbors are considerate. They never play loud music.

   Because my neighbors are considerate, they never play loud music.

1. If the dependent clause comes *before* the main clause, set it off with a comma.

   Before you dive, be sure there is water in the pool.

2. If the dependent clause comes *after* or *within* the main clause, set it off with a comma only if you use the word *though* or *although,* or if the words are not necessary to convey the basic meaning in the sentence.

   Be sure there is water in the pool *before you dive.*

Coordination and Subordination

At times you may want to show the relationship of three or more ideas within one sentence. If that relationship involves two or more main ideas and one or more supporting ideas, the combination can be stated in a **compound-complex sentence** (two or more independent clauses and one or more dependent clauses).

> <u>Before he learned how to operate a computer</u>, <u>he had trouble</u>
>   dependent clause
>
> <u>with his typewritten assignments</u>, but now he <u>produces clean</u>,
>   independent clause   independent clause
>
> <u>attractive material</u>.

Use punctuation consistent with that of the compound and complex sentences.

Other Methods of Combining Ideas

1. Simple sentences can often be combined by using a **prepositional phrase**, a preposition followed by a noun or pronoun object.

   > Dolly Parton wrote a song about a coat. The coat had many colors.
   >
   > Dolly Parton wrote a song about a coat *of many colors.*

2. To combine simple sentences, use an **appositive**, a noun phrase that immediately follows a noun or pronoun and renames it.

   > Susan is the leading scorer on the team. Susan is a quick and strong player.
   >
   > Susan, *a quick and strong player*, is the leading scorer on the? team.

3. Simple sentences can often be combined by dropping a repeated subject in the second sentence.

   > Some items are too damaged for recycling. They must be disposed of.
   >
   > Some items are too damaged for recycling and must be disposed of.

4. Sentences can be combined by using a **participial phrase**, a group of words that include a participle, which is a verb like word that usually ends in *-ing* or *-ed.*

   > John rowed smoothly. He reached the shore.
   >
   > *Rowing smoothly*, John reached the shore.

⌒ Variety in Sentences: Types, Order, Length, Beginnings

Do not bother to look for formulas in this section. Variety in sentences may be desirable for its own sake, to avoid dullness. However, it is more likely you will revise your paragraphs for reasons that make good sense in the context of what you are writing. The following are some of the variations available to you.

Types

You have learned that all four types of sentences are sound. Your task as a writer is to decide which one to use for a particular thought. That decision may not be made until you revise your composition. Then you can choose on the basis of the relationship of ideas:

Simple: a single idea
Compound: two closely related ideas
Complex: one idea more important than the other
Compound-Complex: a combination of compound and complex ideas

These types of sentences were all covered in more detail earlier in this chapter (page 184).

Order

You will choose the order of parts and information according to what you want to emphasize. Typically the most emphatic location is at the end of any unit.

Length

Uncluttered and direct, short sentences commonly draw attention. Because that focus occurs only when they stand out from longer sentences, however, you would usually avoid a series of short sentences.

Beginnings

A long series of sentences with each beginning containing a subject followed by a verb may become monotonous. Consider beginning sentences in different ways:

With a prepositional phrase: *In the distance* a dog barked.
With a transitional connective (conjunctive adverb) such as *then*, *however*, or *therefore*: *Then* the game was over.

With a coordinating conjunction such as *and* or *but*: *But* no
one moved for three minutes.
With a dependent clause: *Although he wanted a new
Corvette,* he settled for a used Ford Taurus.
With an adverb: *Carefully* he removed the thorn from the
lion's paw.

∿ Correcting Fragments, Comma Splices, and Run-Ons

Fragments

A correct sentence signals completeness. Each complete sentence
must have an **independent clause**, meaning a word or a group of
words that contains a subject and a verb that can stand alone.

> *He enrolled* for the fall semester.

A **fragment** (a group of words without a subject, without a verb, or
without both) signals incompleteness—it doesn't make sense. You
would expect the speaker or writer of a fragment to say or write
more or to rephrase it.

1. A **dependent clause**, which begins with a subordinating word,
   cannot stand by itself.

   > *Because* he left.
   >
   > *When* she worked.
   >
   > *Although* they slept.

2. A **verbal phrase**, a **prepositional phrase**, and an **appositive phrase**
   may carry ideas, but each is incomplete because it lacks a subject and a verb.

VERBAL PHRASE	*having studied hard all evening*
SENTENCE	Having studied hard all evening, John decided to retire.
PREPOSITIONAL PHRASE	*in the store*
SENTENCE	She worked in the store.
APPOSITIVE PHRASE	*a successful business*
SENTENCE	Marks Brothers, a successful business, sells clothing.

Comma Splices and Run-Ons

The **comma splice** consists of two independent clauses with only a comma between them.

The weather was disappointing, <u>we canceled the picnic.</u>

A comma by itself cannot join two independent clauses.

The **run-on** differs from the comma splice in only one respect: it has no comma between the independent clauses. Therefore, the run-on is two independent clauses with *nothing* between them.

The weather was disappointing <u>we canceled the picnic.</u>

Independent clauses must be properly connected.

Correct comma splices and run-ons by using a comma and a coordinating conjunction, a subordinating conjunction, or a semi-colon, or by making each clause a separate sentence.

1. Use a comma and a **coordinating conjunction** (*for, and, nor, but, or, yet, so*).

   We canceled the picnic, *for* the weather was disappointing.

2. Use a **subordinating conjunction** (such as *because, after, that, when, although, since, how, until, unless, before*) to make one clause dependent.

   Because the weather was disappointing, we canceled the picnic.

3. Use a **semicolon** (with or without a conjunctive adverb such as *however, otherwise, therefore, similarly, hence, on the other hand, then, consequently, also, thus*).

   The weather was disappointing; we canceled the picnic.

   The weather was disappointing; *therefore,* we canceled the picnic.

4. Make each clause a separate sentence. For a comma splice, replace the comma with a period, and begin the second sentence (clause) with a capital letter. For a run-on, insert a period between the two independent clauses and begin the second sentence with a capital letter.

   The weather was disappointing. We canceled the picnic.

◯ Omissions: When Parts Are Missing

Do not omit words that are needed to make your sentences clear and logical. Of the many types of undesirable constructions in which necessary words are omitted, the following are the most common.

1. **Subjects.** Do not omit a necessary subject in a sentence with two verbs.

ILLOGICAL	The cost of the car was $12,000 but would easily last me through college. (subject of *last*)
LOGICAL	The cost of the car was $12,000, but the car would easily last me through college.

2. **Verbs.** Do not omit verbs that are needed because of a change in the number of the subject or a change of tense.

ILLOGICAL	The bushes were trimmed and the grass mowed.
LOGICAL	The bushes were trimmed, and the grass was mowed.

ILLOGICAL	True honesty always has and always will be admired by most people. (tense)
LOGICAL	True honesty always has been and always will be admired by most people.

3. *That* **as a conjunction.** The conjunction *that* should not be omitted from a dependent clause if there is danger of misreading the sentence.

MISLEADING	We believed Eric, if not stopped, would hurt himself.
CLEAR	We believed that Eric, if not stopped, would hurt himself.

4. **Prepositions.** Do not omit prepositions in idiomatic phrases, in expressions of time, and in parallel phrases.

ILLOGICAL	Weekends the campus is deserted. (time)
LOGICAL	During weekends the campus is deserted.

ILLOGICAL	I have neither love nor patience with untrained dogs. (parallel phrases)
LOGICAL	I have neither love for nor patience with untrained dogs.

ILLOGICAL	Glenda's illness was something we heard only after her recovery.
LOGICAL	Glenda's illness was something we heard about only after her recovery.

∼ Working with Verb Forms

The twelve verb tenses are shown in this section. The irregular verb *drive* is used as the example. (See pages 193–194 for a list of irregular verbs.)

Simple Tenses

Present
I, we, you, they *drive.*
He, she, it *drives.*

May imply
a continuation from
past to future

Past
I, we, you, he, she, it, they *drove.*

Future
I, we, you, he, she, it,
they *will drive.*

Perfect Tenses

Present Perfect
I, we, you, they *have driven.*
He, she, it *has driven.*

Completed recently
in the past, may continue
to the present

Past Perfect
I, we, you, he, she, it, they
had driven.

Completed prior to a
specific time in the past

Future Perfect
I, we, you, he, she, it, they
will have driven.

Will occur at a time
prior to a specific
time in the future

Progressive Tenses

Present Progressive
I *am driving.*
He, she, it *is driving.*
We, you, they *are driving.*

In progress now

Past Progressive
I, he, she, it *was driving.*
We, you, they *were driving.*

In progress in the
past

Future Progressive
I, we, you, he, she, it, they *will be driving.*

In progress in the future

Perfect Progressive Tenses

Present Perfect Progressive
I, we, you, they *have been driving.*
He, she, it *has been driving.*

In progress up to now

Past Perfect Progressive
I, we, you, he, she, it, they *had been driving.*

In progress before another event in the past

Future Perfect Progressive
I, we, you, he, she, it, they *will have been driving.*

In progress before another event in the future

Past Participles

The past participle uses the helping verbs *has, have,* or *had* along with the past tense of the verb. For regular verbs, whose past tense ends in -ed, the past participle form of the verb is the same as the past tense.

Following is a list of some common regular verbs, showing the base form, the past tense, and the past participle. (The base form can also be used with such helping verbs as *can, could, do, does, did, may, might, must, shall, should, will,* and *would.*)

Regular Verbs

Base Form (Present)	Past	Past Participle
ask	asked	asked
answer	answered	answered
cry	cried	cried
decide	decided	decided
dive	dived (dove)	dived
drag	dragged	dragged
finish	finished	finished
happen	happened	happened
learn	learned	learned
like	liked	liked
love	loved	loved
need	needed	needed
open	opened	opened

Base Form (Present)	Past	Past Participle
start	started	started
suppose	supposed	supposed
walk	walked	walked
want	wanted	wanted

Whereas **regular verbs** are predictable—having an *-ed* ending for past and past participle forms—**irregular verbs**, as the term suggests, follow no definite pattern.

Following is a list of some common irregular verbs, showing the base form (present), the past tense, and the past participle.

Irregular Verbs

Base Form (Present)	Past	Past Participle
arise	arose	arisen
awake	awoke (awaked)	awaked
be	was, were	been
become	became	become
begin	began	begun
bend	bent	bent
blow	blew	blown
break	broke	broken
bring	brought	brought
buy	bought	bought
catch	caught	caught
choose	chose	chosen
cling	clung	clung
come	came	come
creep	crept	crept
deal	dealt	dealt
do	did	done
drink	drank	drunk
drive	drove	driven
eat	ate	eaten
feel	felt	felt
fight	fought	fought
fling	flung	flung
fly	flew	flown
forget	forgot	forgotten
freeze	froze	frozen
get	got	got (gotten)
go	went	gone

Base Form (Present)	Past	Past Participle
grow	grew	grown
have	had	had
know	knew	known
lead	led	led
leave	left	left
lose	lost	lost
mean	meant	meant
read	read	read
ride	rode	ridden
ring	rang	rung
see	saw	seen
shine	shone	shone
shoot	shot	shot
sing	sang	sung
sink	sank	sunk
sleep	slept	slept
slink	slunk	slunk
speak	spoke	spoken
spend	spent	spent
steal	stole	stolen
stink	stank (stunk)	stunk
sweep	swept	swept
swim	swam	swum
swing	swung	swung
take	took	taken
teach	taught	taught
tear	tore	torn
think	thought	thought
throw	threw	thrown
wake	woke (waked)	woken (waked)
weep	wept	wept
write	wrote	written

"Problem" Verbs

The following pairs of verbs are especially troublesome and confusing: *lie* and *lay*, *sit* and *set*, and *rise* and *raise*. One way to tell them apart is to remember which word in each pair takes a direct object. A direct object answers the question *whom* or *what* in connection with a verb. The words *lay*, *raise*, and *set* take a direct object.

He *raised* the window. (He *raised* what?)

Lie, rise, and *sit,* however, cannot take a direct object. We cannot say, for example, "He rose the window." In the following examples, the italicized words are objects.

Present Tense	Meaning	Past Tense	Past Participle	Example
lie	to rest	lay	lain	I lay down to rest.
lay	to place something	laid	laid	We laid the *books* on the table.
rise	to go up	rose	risen	The smoke rose quickly.
raise	to lift	raised	raised	She raised the *question.*
sit	to rest	sat	sat	He sat in the chair.
set	to place something	set	set	They set the *basket* on the floor.

Verb Tense

Verb tense is a word form indicating time. The rules about selecting a **tense** for certain kinds of writing are flexible. You should be consistent, however, changing tense only for a good reason.

Usually you should select the present tense to write about literature.

Moby Dick *is* a famous white whale.

Select the past tense to write about yourself (usually) or something historical (always).

I *was* eighteen when I *decided* I *was* ready for independence.

Subject-Verb Agreement

The basic principle of **subject-verb agreement** is that if the subject is singular, the verb should be singular, and if the subject is plural, the verb should be plural. There are ten major guidelines. In the examples under the following guidelines, the true subjects and verbs are italicized.

1. Do not let words that come between the subject and verb affect agreement.

   a. Modifying phrases and clauses frequently come between the subject and verb:

      The various *types* of drama *were* not *discussed.*

      Angela, who is hitting third, *is* the best player.

      The *price* of those shoes *is* too high.

   b. Certain prepositions can cause trouble. The following words are prepositions, not conjunctions: *along with, as well as, besides, in addition to, including,* and *together with.* The words that function as objects of prepositions cannot also be subjects of the sentence.

      The *coach,* along with the players, *protests* the decision.

   c. In compound subjects in which one subject is positive and one subject is negative, the verb agrees with the positive subject.

      Phillip, not the other boys, *was* the culprit.

2. Do not let inversions (verb before subject, not the normal order) affect the agreement of subject and verb.

   a. Verbs and other words may come before the subject. Do not let them affect the agreement. To understand subject-verb relationships, recast the sentence in normal word order.

      Are Juan and his *sister* at home? (question form)

      Juan and his *sister are* at home. (normal order)

   b. A sentence filler is a word that is grammatically independent of other words in the sentence. The most common fillers are *there* and *here.* Even though a sentence filler precedes the verb, it should not be treated as the subject.

      There *are* many *reasons* for his poor work. (The verb *are* agrees with the subject *reasons.*)

3. A singular verb agrees with a singular indefinite pronoun.

   a. Most indefinite pronouns are singular.

      Each of the women *is* ready at this time.

      Neither of the women *is* ready at this time.

      One of the children *is* not paying attention.

b. Certain indefinite pronouns do not clearly express either a singular or plural number. Agreement, therefore, depends on the meaning of the sentence. These pronouns are *all, any, none,* and *some.*

> *All* of the melon *was* good.
>
> *All* of the melons *were* good.
>
> *None* of the pie *is* acceptable.
>
> *None* of the pies *are* acceptable.

4. Two or more subjects joined by *and* usually take a plural verb.

> The *captain* and the *sailors were* happy to be ashore.
>
> The *trees* and *shrubs need* more care.

a. If the parts of a compound subject mean one and the same person or thing, the verb is singular; if the parts mean more than one, the verb is plural.

> The *secretary* and *treasurer is* not present. (one person)
>
> The *secretary* and the *treasurer are* not present. (more than one person)

b. When *each* or *every* modify singular subjects joined by *and,* the verb is singular.

> Each *boy* and each *girl brings* a donation.
>
> Every *woman* and *man has asked* the same questions.

5. Alternative subjects—that is, subjects joined by *or, nor, either/or, neither/nor, not only/but also*—should be handled in the following manner.

a. If the subjects are both singular, the verb is singular.

> *Rosa* or *Alicia is* responsible.

b. If the subjects are plural, the verb is plural.

> Neither the *students* nor the *teachers were* impressed by his comments.

c. If one of the subjects is singular and the other subject is plural, the verb agrees with the nearer subject.

> Either the Garcia *boys* or their *father goes* to the hospital each day.
>
> Either their *father* or the Garcia *boys go* to the hospital each? day.

6. Collective nouns—*team, family, group, crew, gang, class, faculty*, and the like—take a singular verb if the verb is considered a unit, but a plural verb if the group is considered as a number of individuals.

> The *team is playing* well tonight.
>
> The *team are getting* dressed. (Here the individuals are acting not as a unit but separately. If you don't like the way this sounds, rewrite as "The members of the team are getting dressed.")

7. Titles of books, essays, short stories, and plays, a word spoken of as a word, and the names of businesses take a singular verb.

> *The Canterbury Tales was written* by Geoffrey Chaucer.
>
> *Markle Brothers has* a sale this week.

8. Sums of money, distances, and measurements are followed by a singular verb when a unit is meant. They are followed by a plural verb when the individual elements are considered separately.

> *Three dollars was* the price. (unit)
>
> *Three dollars were* lying there. (individual)
>
> *Five years is* a long time. (unit)
>
> The *first five years were* difficult ones. (individual)

9. Be careful of agreement with nouns ending in -*s*. Several nouns ending in -*s* take a singular verb—for example, *aeronautics, civics, economics, ethics, measles,* and *mumps.*

> *Mumps is* an extremely unpleasant disease.
>
> *Economics is* my major field of study.

10. Some nouns have only a plural form and so take only a plural verb—for example, *clothes, fireworks, scissors,* and *pants.*

> His *pants are* badly wrinkled.
>
> Mary's *clothes were* stylish and expensive.

∿ Giving Verbs Voice

Which of these sentences sounds better to you?

> Alex Rodriguez slammed a home run.
>
> A home run was slammed by Alex Rodriguez.

Both sentences carry the same message, but the first expresses it more effectively. The subject (*Alex Rodriguez*) is the actor. The verb (*slammed*) is the action. The direct object (*home run*) is the receiver of the action. The second sentence lacks the vitality of the first because the receiver of the action is the subject; the doer is embedded in the prepositional phrase at the end of the sentence.

The first sentence demonstrates the active voice. It has an active verb (one that leads to a direct object), and the action moves from the beginning to the end of the sentence. The second exhibits the passive voice (with the action reflecting back on the subject). When given a choice, you should usually select the active voice. It promotes energy and directness.

The passive voice, though not usually the preferred form, does have its uses:

- When the doer of the action is unknown or unimportant

  My car was stolen. (The doer, a thief, is unknown.)

- When the receiver of the action is more important than the doer

  My neighbor was permanently disabled by an irresponsible drunk driver. (The neighbor's suffering, not the drunk driver, is the focus.)

As you can see, the passive construction places the doer at the end of a prepositional phrase (as in the second example) or does not include the doer in the statement at all (as in the first example). Instead, the passive voice places the receiver of the action in the subject position, and it presents the verb in its past tense form preceded by a *to be* helper. The transformation is a simple one:

ACTIVE   She read the book.

PASSIVE   The book was read by her.

Because weak sentences often involve the unnecessary and ineffective use of the passive form, you should learn to identify passive constructions and consider changing them to active.

∼ Selecting Pronoun Case

A **pronoun** is a word that is used in place of a noun. **Case** is the form a pronoun takes as it fills a position in a sentence.

1. **Subjective pronouns** are *I*, *he*, and *she* (singular), and *we* and *they* (plural). *Who* can be either singular or plural. Subjective-case pronouns can fill subject positions in a sentence.

   We dance in the park.

   It was *she* who spoke. (referring back to and meaning the same as the subject)

2. **Objective pronouns** are *me*, *him*, and *her* (singular); and *us* and *them* (plural). *Whom* can be either singular or plural. Objective-case pronouns fill object positions.

   We saw *her* in the library. (object of verb)

   They gave the results to *us*—Judy and *me*. (object of a preposition)

3. Three techniques are useful for deciding what pronoun case to use.

   a. If you have a compound element (such as a subject or an object of a preposition), consider only the pronoun part.

      They will visit Jim and (I, me). (*Consider*: They will visit *me*.)

   b. If the next important word after *who* or *whom* in a statement is a noun or pronoun, the word choice will be *whom*; otherwise, it will be *who*. Disregard qualifier clauses such as *It seems* and *I feel*.

      The person *who* works hardest will win.

      The person *whom* judges like will win.

      The person *who*, we think, worked hardest won. (ignoring the qualifier clause)

   c. *Let's* is made up of the words *let* and *us* and means *"you let us"*; therefore, when you select a pronoun to follow it, consider the two original words and select another object word—*me*.

      Let's you and *me* go to town.

Matching Pronouns and Antecedents

A pronoun agrees with its antecedent in person, number, and gender.

1. Avoid needless shifting in **person**, which means shifting in point of view, such as from *I* to *you*.

INCORRECT   *I* tried but *you* couldn't persuade her to return.

CORRECT   *I* tried but *I* couldn't persuade her to return.

2. Most problems with pronoun-antecedent agreement involve number. The principles are simple: If the antecedent (the word the pronoun refers back to) is singular, use a singular pronoun. If the antecedent is plural, use a plural pronoun.

> Jim forgot *his* notebook.
>
> Many students cast *their* votes today.
>
> Someone lost *his* or *her* [not *their*] book.

3. The pronoun should agree with its antecedent in gender, if the gender of the antecedent is specific. Masculine and feminine pronouns are gender-specific: *he, him, she,* and *her.* Others are neuter: *I, we, me, us, it, they, them, who, whom, that,* and *which.* The words *who* and *whom* refer to people. *That* can refer to ideas, things, and people, but usually not to people. *Which* refers to ideas and things, but never to people. To avoid a perceived sex bias, most writers and speakers prefer to use *he or she* or *his or her* instead of just *he* or *his;* however, many writers simply make antecedents plural.

> Everyone should work until *he or she* drops.
>
> People should work until *they* drop.

〰 Using Adjectives and Adverbs

1. **Adjectives** modify (describe) nouns and pronouns and answer the questions *Which one? What kind?* and *How many?*
2. **Adverbs** modify verbs, adjectives, or other adverbs and answer the questions *How? Where? When?* and *To what degree?* Most words ending in *-ly* are adverbs.
3. If you settle for a common word such as *good* or a slang word such as *neat* to characterize something you like, you will be limiting your communication. The more precise the word, the better the communication. Keep in mind, however, that anything can be overdone; therefore, use adjectives and adverbs wisely and economically.
4. For making comparisons, most adjectives and adverbs have three different forms: the positive (one), the comparative (two), and the superlative (three or more).

a. Adjectives

▪ Add *-er* to short adjectives (one or two syllables) to rank units of two.

> Julian is *kinder* than Sam.

▪ Add *-est* to short adjectives (one or two syllables) to rank units of more than two.

> Of the fifty people I know, Julian is the *kindest*.

▪ Add the word *more* before long adjectives to rank units of two.

> My hometown is *more beautiful* than yours.

▪ Add the word *most* before long adjectives to rank units of three or more.

> My hometown is the *most beautiful* in all America.

▪ Some adjectives are irregular in the way they change to show comparison: *good, better, best; bad, worse, worst.*

b. Adverbs

For most adverbs, use the word *more* before the comparative form (two) and the word *most* before the superlative form (three or more).

> Jim performed *skillfully*. (modifier)
>
> Joan performed *more skillfully* than Morton. (comparative modifier)
>
> But Susan performed *most skillfully* of all. (superlative modifier)

5. Avoid double negatives. Words such as *no, not, none, nothing, never, hardly, barely,* and *scarcely* should not be combined.

> INCORRECT   I *don't* have *no* time for recreation.
> CORRECT   I have *no* time for recreation.
> CORRECT   I *don't* have time for recreation.

6. Do not confuse adjectives (*bad*) with adverbs (*badly*).

> INCORRECT   I feel *badly* about being late.
> CORRECT   I feel *bad* about being late.
> INCORRECT   He handled the situation *bad*.
> CORRECT   He handled the situation *badly*.

Eliminating Dangling and Misplaced Modifiers

1. A modifier that gives information but doesn't refer to a word or group of words already in the sentence is called a **dangling modifier**.

    DANGLING *Walking down the street,* a snake startled me.

    CORRECT *Walking down the street,* I was startled by a snake.

2. A modifier that is placed so that it modifies the wrong word or words is called a **misplaced modifier**.

    MISPLACED The sick man went to a doctor *with a high fever.*

    CORRECT The sick man with a high fever went to a doctor.

Balancing Sentence Parts

1. **Parallelism** means balancing one structure with another of the same kind—nouns with nouns, verbs with verbs, adjectives (words that can describe nouns) with adjectives, adverbs (words that can describe verbs) with adverbs, and so forth.

    Men, women, and *children* [nouns] *enjoy* the show and *return* [verbs] each year.

    She fell *in love* and *out of love* [prepositional phrases] in a few seconds.

    She fell in love with him, and *he fell in love with her* [clauses].

2. Faulty parallel structure is awkward and draws unfavorable attention to what is being said.

    To talk with his buddies and *eating* fast foods were his favorite pastimes. (The sentence should be *Talking . . .* and *eating* or *To talk . . .* and *to eat.*)

3. Some words signal parallel structure. All coordinating conjunctions (*for, and, nor, but, or, yet, so*) can give such signals.

    The weather is hot *and* humid.

    He purchased a Dodger Dog, *but* I chose Stadium Peanuts.

4. Combination words also signal the need for parallelism or balance. The most common combination words are *either/or, neither/nor, not only/but also, both/and,* and *whether/or.*

    We will *either* win this game *or* go out fighting. (verb following each of the combination words)

⌒ Avoiding Wordy Phrases

Certain phrases clutter sentences, consuming our time in writing and our readers' time in reading. Watch for wordy phrases as you revise and edit.

WORDY   *Due to the fact that* he was unemployed, he had to use public transportation.

CONCISE *Because* he was unemployed, he had to use public transportation.

WORDY   *Deep down inside* he believed that the Red Sox would win.

CONCISE He believed that the Red Sox would win.

Wordy	Concise
at the present time	now
basic essentials	essentials
blend together	blend
it is clear that	(delete)
due to the fact that	because
for the reason that	because
I felt inside	I felt
in most cases	usually
as a matter of fact	in fact
in the event that	if
until such time as	until
I personally feel	I feel
in this modern world	today
in order to	to
most of the people	most people
along the lines of	like
past experience	experience
at that point in time	then
in the final analysis	finally
in the near future	soon
have a need for	need
in this day and age	now

〜 Mastering Punctuation

1. The three marks of end punctuation are periods, question marks, and exclamation points.

   a. Periods

   Place a period after a statement.
   Place a period after common abbreviations.

   Use an ellipsis—three periods within a sentence and four periods at the end of a sentence—to indicate that words have been omitted from quoted material.

   > He stopped walking and the buildings . . . rose up out of the misty courtroom. . . . (James Thurber, "The Secret Life of Walter Mitty")

   b. Question marks

   Place a question mark at the end of a direct question.
   Use a single question mark in sentence constructions that contain a double question—that is, a quoted question within a question.

   > Mr. Martin said, "Did he say, 'Are we going?'"

   Do *not* use a question mark after an indirect (reported) question.

   > She asked me what caused the slide.

   c. Exclamation points

   Place an exclamation point after a word or group of words that expresses strong feeling.
   Do not overwork the exclamation point. Do not use double exclamation points.

2. The comma is used essentially to separate and to set off sentence elements.

   a. Use a comma to separate main clauses joined by one of the coordinating conjunctions—*for, and, nor, but, or, yet, so.*

   > We went to the game, *but* it was canceled.

   b. Use a comma after introductory dependent clauses and long introductory phrases (generally, four or more words is considered long).

   > *Before she and I arrived*, the meeting was called to order.

c. Use a comma to separate words, phrases, and clauses in a series.

> He ran *down the street, across the park,* and *into the arms* of his father.

d. Use a comma to separate coordinate adjectives not joined by *and* that modify the same noun.

> I need a *sturdy, reliable* truck.

e. Use a comma to separate sentence elements that might be misread.

> *Inside,* the dog scratched his fleas.

f. Use commas to set off (enclose) nonessential (unnecessary for meaning of the sentence) words, phrases, and clauses.

> Maria, *who studied hard,* will pass.

g. Use commas to set off parenthetical elements such as mild interjections (*oh, well, yes, no,* and others), most conjunctive adverbs (*however, otherwise, therefore, similarly, hence, on the other hand,* and *consequently,* but not *then, thus, soon, now,* and *also*), quotation indicators, and special abbreviations (*etc., i.e., e.g.,* and others).

> *Oh,* what a silly question! (mild interjection)
>
> It is necessary, *of course,* to leave now. (sentence modifier)
>
> We left early; *however,* we missed the train anyway. (conjunctive adverb)
>
> "When I was in school," *he said,* "I read widely." (quotation indicator)
>
> Books, papers, pens, *etc.,* were scattered on the floor. (The abbreviation *etc.,* however, should be used sparingly.)

h. Use commas to set off nouns used as direct address.

> Play it again, *Sam.*

i. Use commas to separate the numbers in a date.

> June *4, 1965,* is a day I will remember.

j. Use commas to separate the city from the state. No comma is used between the state and the zip code.

> Walnut, CA 91789

k. Use a comma following the salutation and the complementary closing in a letter (but in a business letter, use a colon after the salutation).

> Dear John,
>
> Sincerely,

l. Use a comma in numbers to set off groups of three digits. However, omit the comma in dates and in long serial numbers, page numbers, and street numbers.

> The total assets were *$2,000,000.*
>
> I was born in 1989.

3. The semicolon indicates a stronger division than the comma. It is used principally to separate independent clauses within a sentence.

a. Use a semicolon to separate independent clauses not joined by a coordinating conjunction.

> You must buy that car today; tomorrow will be too late.

b. Use a semicolon between two independent clauses joined by a conjunctive adverb (such as *however, otherwise, therefore, similarly, hence, on the other hand, then, consequently, accordingly, thus*).

> It was very late; *therefore,* I remained at the hotel.

4. Quotation marks bring special attention to words.

a. Quotation marks are used principally to set off direct quotations. A direct quotation consists of material taken from the written work or the direct speech of others; it is set off by double quotation marks. Single quotation marks are used to set off a quotation within a quotation.

> He said, "I don't remember if she said, 'Wait for me.'"

b. Use double quotation marks to set off titles of shorter pieces of writing such as magazine articles, essays, short stories, short poems, one-act plays, chapters in books, songs, and separate pieces of writing published as part of a larger work.

> The book *Literature: Structure, Sound, and Sense* contains a deeply moving poem titled "On Wenlock Edge."

Have you read "The Use of Force," a short story by William Carlos Williams?

My favorite Elvis song is "Don't Be Cruel."

c. Punctuation with quotation marks follows definite rules.

- A period or comma is always placed *inside* the quotation marks.

  Our assignment for Monday was to read Poe's "The Raven."

  "I will read you the story," he said. "It is a good one."

- A semicolon or colon is always placed *outside* the quotation marks.

  He read Robert Frost's poem "Design"; then he gave the examination.

- A question mark, an exclamation point, or a dash is placed *outside* the quotation marks when it applies to the entire sentence and *inside* the quotation marks when it applies to the material in quotation marks.

  He asked, "Am I responsible for everything?" (quoted question within a statement)

  Did you hear him say, "I have the answer"? (statement within a question)

  Did she say, "Are we ready?" (question within a question)

  She shouted, "Impossible!" (exclamation)

  "I hope—that is, I—" he began. (dash)

5. Italics (slanting type) is used to call special attention to certain words or groups of words. In handwriting, such words are <u>underlined</u>.

   a. Italicize (underline) foreign words and phrases that are still listed in the dictionary as foreign.

      c'est la vie   Weltschmerz

   b. Italicize (underline) titles of books (except the Bible); long poems; plays; magazines; motion pictures; musical compositions; newspapers; works of art; names of aircraft; ships; and letters, figures, and words referred to by their own name.

      War and Peace   Apollo 12   leaving *o* out of *sophomore*

6. The dash is used when a stronger break than the comma is needed. It can also be used to indicate a break in the flow of thought and to emphasize words (less formal than the colon in this situation).

> Here is the true reason—but maybe you don't care.
>
> English, French, history—these are the subjects I like.

7. The colon is a formal mark of punctuation used chiefly to introduce something that is to follow, such as a list, a quotation, or an explanation.

> These cars are my favorites: Cadillac, Chevrolet, Buick, Oldsmobile, and Pontiac.

8. Parentheses are used to set off material that is of relatively little importance to the main thought of the sentence. Such material—numbers that designate items in a series, figures, supplementary material, and sometimes explanatory details—merely amplifies the main thought.

> The years of the era (1961–1973) were full of action.
>
> Her husband (she had been married only a year) died last week.

9. Brackets are used within a quotation to set off editorial additions or corrections made by the person who is quoting.

> Churchill said: "It [the Yalta Agreement] contained many mistakes."

10. The apostrophe is used with nouns and indefinite pronouns to show possession; to show the omission of letters and figures in contractions; and to form the plurals of letters, figures, and words referred to as words.

> man's coat   girls' clothes
>
> you're (contraction of *you are*)   five *and*'s

11. The hyphen brings two or more words together into a single compound word. Correct hyphenation, therefore, is essentially a spelling problem rather than one of punctuation. Because the hyphen is not used with any degree of consistency, consult your dictionary for current usage. Study the following as a beginning guide.

a. Use a hyphen to separate the parts of many compound words.

> about-face   go-between

b. Use a hyphen between prefixes and proper names.

>   all-American   mid-November

c. Use a hyphen to join two or more words used as a single adjective modifier before a noun.

>   first-class service   hard-fought game
>   sad-looking mother

d. Use a hyphen with spelled-out compound numbers up to ninety-nine and with fractions.

>   twenty-six   two-thirds

Note: Dates, street addresses, numbers requiring more than two words, chapter and page numbers, time followed directly by *a.m.* or *p.m.*, and figures after a dollar sign or before measurement abbreviations are usually written as figures, not words.

Conquering Capitalization

In English, there are many conventions concerning the use of capital letters. Here are some of them.

1. Capitalize the first word of a sentence.
2. Capitalize proper nouns and adjectives derived from proper nouns.

- Names of persons
  >   Edward Jones
- Adjectives derived from proper nouns
  >   a Shakespearean sonnet   a Miltonic sonnet
- Countries, nationalities, races, and languages
  >   Germany   English   Spanish   Chinese
- States, regions, localities, and other geographical divisions
  >   California   the Far East   the South
- Oceans, lakes, mountains, deserts, streets, and parks
  >   Lake Superior   Sahara Desert   Fifth Avenue
- Educational institutions, schools, and courses
  >   Santa Ana College   Joe Hill School
  >   Rowland High School   Spanish 3
- Organizations and their members
  >   Boston Red Sox   Audubon Society   Boy Scouts

- Corporations, governmental agencies or departments, trade names
  > U.S. Steel Corporation   Treasury Department
  > White Memorial Library   Coke
- Calendar references such as holidays, days of the week, months
  > Easter   Tuesday   January
- Historic eras, periods, documents, laws
  > First Crusade   Romantic Age
  > Declaration of Independence   Geneva Convention

3. Capitalize words denoting family relationships when they are used before a name or substituted for a name.

   > He walked with his nephew and Aunt Grace.
   >
   > *but*
   >
   > He walked with his nephew and his aunt.

   > Grandmother and Mother are away on vacation.
   >
   > *but*
   >
   > My grandmother and my mother are away on vacation.

4. Capitalize abbreviations after names.

   > Henry White Jr.   William Green, M.D.

5. Capitalize titles of themes, books, plays, movies, poems, magazines, newspapers, musical compositions, songs, and works of art. Do not capitalize short conjunctions and prepositions unless they come at the beginning or the end of the title.

   > *Desire Under the Elms*   *Terminator*
   > *Last of the Mohicans*   *Of Mice and Men*
   > "Blueberry Hill"

6. Capitalize any title preceding a name or used as a substitute for a name. Do not capitalize a title following a name.

   > Judge Stone   Alfred Stone, a judge
   > General Clark   Raymond Clark, a general
   > Professor Fuentes   Harry Jones, the former president

Index